Mary Elise Sarotte

German Military Reform and European Security

Adelphi Paper 340

Oxford University Press, Great Clarendon Street, Oxford OX2 6DP
Oxford New York
Athens Auckland Bangkok Bombay Calcutta Cape Town
Dar es Salaam Delhi Florence Hong Kong Istanbul Karachi
Kuala Lumpur Madras Madrid Melbourne Mexico City
Nairobi Paris Singapore Taipei Tokyo Toronto
and associated companies in
Berlin Ibadan

Oxford is a trade mark of Oxford University Press

Published in the United States
by Oxford University Press Inc., New York

© The International Institute for Strategic Studies 2001

First published October 2001 by **Oxford University Press** for
The International Institute for Strategic Studies
Arundel House, 13–15 Arundel Street, Temple Place, London WC2R 3DX
www.iiss.org

Director John Chipman
Editor Mats R. Berdal
Assistant Editor Jennifer Knight
Design and Production Shirley Nicholls

British Library Cataloguing in Publication Data
Data available

Library of Congress Cataloguing in Publication Data

ISBN 0-19-851564-2
ISSN 0567-932x

Contents

Tables

Glossary

ABM	Anti-Ballistic Missile
CC	Command and Control
CCC	Capabilities Commitment Conference
CDU	Christian Democratic Union
CFSP	Common Foreign and Security Policy (of the EU)
CJTF	Combined Joint Task Force
COPS	French acronym for EU political and security committee
COTS	Commercial Off-The-Shelf Technology
CSU	Christian Social Union
CTBT	Comprehensive Test Ban Treaty
DCI	Defence Capabilities Initiative
DM	Deployability and Mobility
DM	Deutschmark (German currency)
EADS	European Aeronautic, Defence and Space Company
EE	Effective Engagement
ESDP	European Security and Defence Policy
EU	European Union
EUMS	EU Military Staff
FDP	Free Democratic Party
FLA	Future Large Aircraft
GDP	Gross Domestic Product
HG	Headline Goal
HTF	Headline Goal Task Force (HTF+ when meeting with NATO experts)

KFOR	Kosovo Force
LOI	Letter of Intent
MC	Military Committee
MOU	Memorandum of Understanding
NATO	North Atlantic Treaty Organisation
NMD	National Missile Defense
NVA	German Acronym for East German People's Army
SEAD	Suppression of Enemy Air Defences
SF	Survivability of Forces and Infrastructure
SL	Sustainability and Logistics
SPD	German acronym for Social Democratic Party of Germany
UN	United Nations
WEU	West European Union

Introduction

Since the fall of the Berlin Wall in 1989, the *Bundeswehr* has faced, and mastered, a series of singular situations: unexpected reunification of East and West Germany; the imperative to absorb the East German People's Army (NVA); and the calls for German out-of-area deployments in crisis areas. Yet, despite successfully responding to all of these challenges, the *Bundeswehr* has still to master another formidable obstacle: reforming itself.

To overcome this obstacle, the *Bundeswehr* will have to go through a difficult process of evolution. The extent of the transformation needed becomes clearer when set in its historical context. Not surprisingly, after the Second World War the leaders of the time, both domestic and foreign, were determined to create a new kind of West German military force, one that could never again unleash suffering on its neighbours. There would be no general staff as commonly construed in the West. Rather, the *Bundeswehr* would serve as a kind of headless force under NATO command. Parliamentary control of the military was firmly established, as was an aversion to 'interventionism'. Throughout the Cold War, the West German public perceived NATO as an instrument for organising Allied defence of West German territory. A 'culture of reticence' came to characterise the country's attitude towards use of military force for any purposes other than territorial defence.[1]

The end of the Cold War demanded a replacement of these outdated views – but with what? The opaque nature of the threats that a new and united Germany had to confront – instead of Soviet divisions, it now faced economic instability in the former Warsaw Pact countries and ethnic rivalries in the Balkans – complicated matters further. On top of this, in July 1994, the German Constitutional Court ruled that there was in fact no constitutional bar to the use of German armed forces abroad. It became apparent, as RAND concluded, that 'the question of the future role of the *Bundeswehr* in new NATO missions [was] no longer one of *whether* but of *when* and *how* [author's italics].'[2]

Gradually, German defence ministers, notably Volker Rühe, initiated the delicate process of reaccustoming the German public – not to mention Germany's neighbours – to German military action beyond the territory of NATO. *Bundeswehr* soldiers and airmen participated in various UN missions. In 1992–93, a small group of 448 Germans worked in UN hospitals in Cambodia. Between 1992 and 1994, a larger group of approximately 1,800 soldiers joined the UN in Somalia. German helicopters also flew for the UN Special Commission on Disarmament (UNSCOM) in Iraq in the period 1992–96. From 1993 to 1995, as part of NATO missions, nearly 500 German troops took part in *Operation Deny Flight* over Bosnia. Further contingents participated in Balkan ground deployments after the Dayton Accords in late 1995.[3]

Finally, *Operation Allied Force*, the 78-day air war against Serbia in the spring of 1999, showed that the once unthinkable had become the expected – and also that a centre-left government would not undo Rühe's work. In 1999, the new coalition government, under Gerhard Schröder of the Social Democratic Party (SPD) and Foreign Minister Joschka Fischer of the Green Party, secured parliamentary approval for German participation in Kosovo, despite public concern about involvement in combat missions in a historically sensitive area. Nor did German participation in Kosovo cease with the end of hostilities; by the summer of 2000, the 8,000-strong contribution to peacekeeping in the Balkans represented the second largest in NATO.[4] A German general, Klaus Reinhardt, performed a tour of duty as commander of the Kosovo Force (KFOR). Defence Minister Rudolf Scharping is also on the record as being committed to maintaining the German presence there for the long term, cautioning in the year 2000 that even 'five years would be clearly too short a time'.[5] In short, these steps represented a major transition for a country that as recently as 1990 was still technically an occupied country itself.

The latest challenge for the *Bundeswehr* is the EU commitment to establishing a European Security and Defence Policy (ESDP), which is forcing the *Bundeswehr* to confront its unique founding charter. Because of ESDP, the German military is under pressure to become, once again, an interventionist force. In many ways, this transition represents a bigger challenge than the practicalities of unification, or of absorbing the NVA.

One cannot separate the prospects for German military reform from the prospects for the success of ESDP as a whole.[6] The ability of the 15 EU member states, together with their key neighbours and allies, to create a viable ESDP depends to a large extent on the ability of the three main players – France, the United Kingdom and Germany – to provide the necessary men and materiel.[7] While all three countries are currently restructuring their armed forces in order to meet the challenges of the future, it is Germany that has the furthest to go.

In recognition of this, Gerhard Schröder's cabinet voted unanimously in the summer of 2000 to begin an ambitious process of reform. After a brief public discussion of various initial proposals in May and June 2000, the cabinet approved Defence Minister Rudolf Scharping's reform outline (excerpts of the initial proposals, and Scharping's own, are provided in the Appendix). Scharping then instructed his staff to prepare a rough outline, or *Grobausplanung*, in the autumn of 2000, followed in January 2001 by the more detailed *Feinausplanung*. As planning ends and implementation begins, it is a good time to assess the reform so far, and what it implies for the future of the *Bundeswehr* and European security ambitions in general. To this end, this paper is structured around three basic questions:

- What is the *context* of German military reform, and what impact does it have on German decision-making?
- What is the *content* of *Bundeswehr* reform as announced and implemented so far?
- What are the likely *consequences* of *Bundeswehr* reform for Germany's NATO allies and, specifically, for ESDP?

A central argument running through the paper is that the current course and potential outcomes of German military reform can only be understood against the background of a historical and societal context unique to Germany. The *Bundeswehr* must overcome its founding charter as a non-interventionist, conscription-based territorial defence force. In trying to implement reform, however, Germans remain painfully cognisant of historical concerns about the danger of creating a fully professional, interventionist military. Such worries naturally arise from the unique role of Germany as the ultimate source of not one, but two world wars. There is also concern about the financial health of Germany, which again has historical roots. Such historical worries, while understandable, nonetheless create obstacles to modernising the *Bundeswehr*.

It must be emphasised that both in word (the stated intentions of *Bundeswehr* reform planners) and in deed (the German presence in Kosovo), German leaders are making a substantial effort to implement military reform. Hence, the problem is not so much the stated content of the military reform plans. Germany has indeed come a long way from the Cold War 'culture of reticence'. Rather, the problem is twofold – it lies partly in faulty execution (most importantly inadequate financing), and partly in the conflicting priorities set for reform by German political leaders. Even as German policy-makers say that the goal of restructuring is to increase Germany's effectiveness as an ally to its EU partners and to NATO, a prioritisation of German domestic concerns paradoxically undercuts this aim.

In practical terms, this means that German defence planners still firmly believe that it is essential to devote scarce military funds to an abbreviated (and potentially intermittent) basic training programme for conscripts in order to provide territorial defence against a potential threat arising from instability in Russia. The majority of Germans view conscription as a necessary safeguard against the risks that a 'professional military' may pose to civil society. A corollary is the notion that large numbers of small, scattered bases are essential to maintaining widespread contact between the military and society at large. This is vital (Germans argue) to maintaining healthy civil–military relations.

Moreover, German military experts disdain the commonly held notion that a conscript army is not a 'professional' army; they do not view the words 'professional' and 'conscript' as antonyms, as do their counterparts in Paris, London and Washington. Indeed, the tendency of German politicians, military leaders and journalists to denigrate the qualities of professional soldiers is causing unnecessary friction with those countries that do have professional forces. There is a popular assumption in Germany, as Chapter One will discuss, that the kind of men and women who would voluntarily serve in a professional military must be 'Rambos, rightists and idiots', in the words of the weekly magazine, *Der Spiegel*.

For their part, policy-makers in London, Paris and Washington mistakenly view the determination of political leaders in Berlin to maintain conscription as bowing to the pressure of public opinion, often assuming that their German counterparts are engaged in an uphill battle against a misguided, uninformed public. Americans in particular see German public sentiment in this regard as an issue to be changed via political leadership. These policy-makers are forgetting the continuing importance in Germany of the historical argument that a professional military is dangerous, a potential rogue state within the state. German policy-makers and analysts agree with public sentiment regarding conscription, or at the very least see no reason to make energetic efforts to combat it. Interest among German leaders in shifting the domestic terms of the debate to bring them more in line with opinion in Washington, London and Paris is limited.

Such German domestic considerations require recognition in both bilateral and institutional contacts with Germany, for they are increasingly becoming a source of resentment. Instead of wondering why German leaders do not campaign against the draft more assertively, Germany's key allies need to accept that Berlin does not view abolition of conscription as the 'right answer' to the challenge of the post-Cold War security environment. Rather, Germans see many convincing reasons why conscripts are still a necessary and useful part of its force structure. This difference of opinion is but one of many. Understanding these differences is essential to understanding the context and content of German military reform, as well as its consequences for ESDP.

The EU hopes, with ESDP, to create its own capacity to face a wide range of challenges – not just the so-called Petersberg tasks (outlined in the Western European Union (WEU) Petersberg Declaration of 1992 as rescue tasks, humanitarian aid, crisis management, peacekeeping and peacemaking) but 'Petersberg-plus'. But the EU is currently heading for 'Petersberg-minus'. Why? This paper will develop in detail the following argument. In order to live up to its full potential, ESDP requires Britain, France and Germany to participate fully in security challenges requiring force projection. Yet Berlin has not convincingly shown that its military reform will give Germany the ability to do so. Rather, *Bundeswehr* reform to date has prioritised German domestic concerns – particularly financing, conscription and threat assessment – over European and NATO preferences. While understandable from a German political point of view, this prioritisation nonetheless means that the modernisation of the *Bundeswehr* will fail to live up to its allies' expectations.

Chapter 1

The Context of the Security Debate in Germany

Karsten Voigt, long one of the SPD's senior foreign-policy figures, likes to explain the differences between British, French and German modes of dealing with Americans as follows. In reply to an American request, a Briton will first respond 'yes' in public, then later add 'yes, but ...' in private. A Frenchman replies 'no' in public, then adds 'no, but ...' in private. Germans, however, respond 'yes' in public, 'yes' in private, and then go home and complain about how arrogant the Americans are.

This anecdote illuminates more than the nature of US–German relations. Germans use among themselves different terms and concepts about security issues than do Americans, or the French or British. Both the actual terms used in discussions about the future of the *Bundeswehr* and the range of opinions on how best to ensure German and European security are notably different in Berlin than in London, Paris or Washington, even considering the disagreements that exist between the latter three. While the differences between Germany and its allies may not be drastic enough to threaten the transatlantic alliance, they are real and non-trivial and have received insufficient attention. They may be summarised and discussed under five headings:

- lack of a sense of urgency;
- resistance to pressure from abroad;
- limited top-level interest;

- sustained support for conscription; and
- differing risk prioritisation.

Lack of a Sense of Urgency

When discussing security matters in Germany, as opposed to the US, the first difference to become apparent is the lack of urgency in the German debate.[1] While few EU members can be accused of excessive zeal when it comes to defence reform, the issue assumes a particular character in Germany. The reason lies in Germany's former role as the 'front-line' Cold War state. Compared to that unhappy situation, even considering the September 2001 terrorist attacks, Germany's current strategic position seems to both the public and the policy-making élite to be an improvement. As a report prepared under the leadership of the former president, Richard von Weizsäcker, put it, 'For the first time in its history, Germany is surrounded on all sides solely by allies and integration partners and faces no threat to its territory from neighbours. This new basis of German security is not of a transitory nature, but will remain valid for the foreseeable future.'[2] It is not uncommon to find the German press referring to the 'disappearance of strategic threats' to the Federal Republic.[3]

This attitude contrasted sharply with the sense in Washington, even before 11 September, that the post-Cold War period had brought new and less well-understood challenges (such as biological, chemical, terrorist and cyber-warfare threats) to add to the still existing old Cold War concerns about nuclear proliferation. This discrepancy in threat perception made front-page headlines during the May 2001 meeting of NATO foreign ministers in Budapest. *The International Herald Tribune,* for example, reported that France and Germany in particular 'did not feel endangered … [or] deem it wise to provoke a potential confrontation by declaring that they were'.[4] As a result, policy-makers in Berlin do not have the same sense of urgency regarding military reform felt most keenly in Washington, but also to an extent in Paris and London. In contrast to the feeling of insecurity in the US, where the Bush administration was already seeking a dramatic extension of its defence plans to include space-based systems even before 11 September, and in contrast to the desire of both the British and French to modernise their militaries, Germans stick to their old model of continuity and consensual evolution when discussing security matters. German politicians are especially fervent proponents of the European penchant for slow, rolling consensus-building.

When it works well, as in the way German governments in the 1990s fostered acceptance of German force projection, such consensus-building helps to bring about change without disruption. For example, the gradual increase in both the number and extent of German deployments over the 1990s was well-paced (and fortunate in that no great mishaps occurred in the course of them).[5] Both the previous Christian Democratic Union (CDU) administrations and the current red–green coalition have slowly but successfully created political *will* for German force projection. While *will* is not a synonym for *capacity* for force projection, it is nonetheless a necessary precursor.

Hence, given the track record of success on this issue of will, Germans prefer to adhere to the gradualist approach. This preference arises not only from a differing threat assessment, but also from the sense that Germany can only handle a limited amount of dramatic change all at once. There was, after all, no shortage of change in Germany over the course of the 1990s. Apart from the obvious shift from a divided to a unified state, there were a number of other significant transitions. In 1998, for the first time, an election (as opposed to parliamentary votes of no-confidence) caused the replacement of a right-of-centre with a left-of-centre government. Shortly thereafter, nearly all decision-making components of the federal government and civil service moved from Bonn to Berlin. Then, in 1999, came the startling revelations about the financial misdeeds of a man viewed as one of Germany's greatest statesmen, Helmut Kohl. In light of these changes, the desire for continuity where possible remains strong.

However, because of the pressure to fulfil NATO's Defence Capabilities Initiative (DCI) and to create a strengthened ESDP, it is becoming apparent that the gradual approach is not the best one for the current challenges. It creates resentment at a time when Germany's allies, especially the US in the wake of the terrorist attacks, wish to move more quickly. An unfortunate dynamic thereby arises, with the US putting pressure on Germany, while Germany resists calls for faster movement on DCI. Washington demands that Berlin live up to its pre-existing agreements, both to its EU partners and to NATO. In return, the German Defence Ministry bristles at American talk about 'forcing' Germany to face realities. As one senior official testily put it, America 'cannot *force* us to do anything'.[6]

Resistance to Pressure from Abroad

It is not only the US, however, that faces this problem. Indeed, US pressure is not any more counter-productive than pressure on Germany from its European allies. They are both counter-productive. How Germany fulfils its commitments to its allies is, according many German officials, up to Germany, as long as it does fulfil them; its allies should refrain from dispensing advice too freely.

Germans are, unfortunately, particularly resistant to the terms that their key allies often employ. Prime examples are calls from allies for the *Bundeswehr* to increase its ability to participate in 'interventions' in crisis areas. Given German military history, the word 'intervention' carries extremely negative implications. In fact, it serves as potent political criticism in the mouths of opponents of military deployments. This dynamic is a key factor in the reform process, because it leads to friction and decreased German willingness to listen to the concerns of its allies.

These negative connotations particularly decrease the value of British military advice in German eyes, since the British military is viewed as a classically over-ambitious 'interventionist' force. Mid-level officers in Germany who deal with the practicalities of day-to-day contacts with NATO display only limited interest in British styles and methods as guidelines for the *Bundeswehr*.

Exacerbating this dim view of the British military tradition is Germany's prioritisation of the French–German partnership, although relations across the Rhine did decay notably in the first half of 2001 after Berlin and Paris disagreed sharply at the Nice summit in December 2000. The summit clearly revealed the strains in the special relationship, particularly the waning German willingness to clear its policy initiatives with France before advancing them to the broader EU. However, this did not lead to a compensatory warming of British–German relations (only the sense that the UK had perhaps gained a bit more freedom of action in European matters). Post-Nice agreements to institute bilateral Franco-German consultations every six to eight weeks, as opposed to twice yearly, might help to improve matters.[7]

Germans are further resistant to what they consider the unjust and inaccurate practice of assessing defence spending as a percentage of gross domestic product (GDP). They resent, in particular, the tendency to quote the percentage of GDP that Germany spends on the

Table 1 International Comparisons of Defence Expenditure and Military Manpower, 1985, 1999 and 2000

| Constant 1999 US$ | Defence Expenditure | | | | | | | | | Numbers in Armed Forces (000) | |
| | US$m | | | US$ per capita | | | % of GDP | | | | |
	1985	1999	2000	1985	1999	2000	1985	1999	2000	1985	2000
Canada	11,597	8,395	7,456	457	275	239	2.2	1.3	1.2	83.0	59.1
US	382,548	292,147	294,695	1,599	1,061	1,059	6.5	3.2	3.0	2,151.6	1,365.8
NATO Europe											
Belgium	6,100	3,442	3,335	619	339	328	3.0	1.4	1.4	91.6	39.3
Czech Republic	n.a.	1,155	1,133	n.a.	112	111	n.a.	2.2	2.2	n.a.	57.7
Denmark	3,098	2,661	2,401	606	504	454	2.2	1.6	1.5	29.6	21.8
France	48,399	37,811	34,292	877	642	580	4.0	2.8	2.6	464.3	294.4
Germany	52,246	31,182	28,229	688	380	343	3.2	1.6	1.6	478.0	221.1
Greece	3,451	5,206	5,457	347	491	513	7.0	4.8	4.9	201.5	159.2
Hungary	3,517	768	777	330	76	77	7.2	1.6	1.7	106.0	43.8
Iceland	n.a.	n.a.	n.a.	n.a.	n.a.	n.a.	n.a.	n.a.	n.a.	n.a.	n.a.
Italy	25,459	22,664	20,561	446	395	359	2.3	2.0	1.9	385.1	250.6
Luxembourg	95	135	126	258	316	291	0.9	0.8	0.8	0.7	0.8
Netherlands	8,812	6,193	6,392	608	394	405	3.1	1.6	1.9	105.5	51.9
Norway	3,067	3,241	2,856	738	730	640	3.1	2.2	1.8	37.0	26.7
Poland	8,533	3,222	3,191	229	83	82	8.1	2.0	2.0	319.0	217.3
Portugal	1,816	2,302	2,197	178	233	222	3.1	2.1	2.2	73.0	44.7
Spain	11,164	7,227	7,053	289	183	178	2.4	1.3	1.3	320.0	166.0
Turkey	3,401	9,717	10,609	68	148	159	4.5	5.2	5.2	630.0	609.7
United Kingdom	47,240	36,368	33,894	835	619	576	5.2	2.5	2.4	334.0	212.5
Subtotal NATO Europe	226,397	173,291	162,503	475	353	332	4.0	2.2	2.2	3,575.3	2,417.5
Total NATO	620,542	473,834	464,654	540	388	368	4.0	2.2	2.2	5,809.9	3,842.4

Source: The Military Balance 2001–02 (IISS, October 2001).

Bundeswehr as a measure of German military capabilities.

The numbers are indeed discouraging. In 2000, the UK and France spent 2.4% and 2.6% respectively of their GDP on defence, while Germany only spent 1.6%. As for research and development, in constant 1999 US dollars, German spending has decreased from $1.547 billion in 1997 to $1.286bn in 2001; French levels were $3.975bn and $3.145bn in 1997 and 2001 respectively, while British levels showed a real increase from $3.632bn to $3.986bn. Defence experts estimate that the cumulative defence-investment backlog has now reached an amount between DM15–19bn, and that annual defence expenditures would have to be increased by at least 10% to make up for the shortfall, unless matching funds are found through cuts in other areas. And this is despite the fact that the German economy grew by 3% in 2000, the strongest rate since 1992.

However, Gerhard Schröder's security advisers tend to dismiss such complaints about German defence spending as a percentage of GDP. They consider the figures to be misleading, because 'defence spending' contains different components in different countries. The French budget includes the *gendarmerie*, but the German budget does not. These numbers, in Schröder's view, also ignore spending that has security implications but is not included in the defence budget, such as the aid that Germany gives not only to the former East Germany but also to the former Soviet Union. For example, in the years 1990–93 Germany provided $8bn in assistance to the Russian armed forces during their withdrawal from Germany. Scharping's ministry also received an extra-budgetary DM2bn, renewed for the coming year. These funds were allocated to cover costs related to the military deployment in Kosovo. Berlin views these as examples of significant contributions to the cause of European security that occur outside of the defence budget. It feels that its allies do not sufficiently remember or credit such contributions. What will count, emphasises the Chancellery, will be the results, not comparisons of figures.[8]

Limited Top-Level Interest

A further unique attribute of security discussions in Berlin lies in the status of these issues in the eyes of Gerhard Schröder. In contrast to, say, Tony Blair or Jacques Chirac, security issues do not usually head Schröder's priority list, although the events of 11 September did make them top priority for nearly every NATO head of government. Nor does foreign policy play the same role in domestic elections throughout the West as it did during the Cold War. On the other hand, Schröder's predecessor was a major figure in international diplomacy. Hence the perception of a disparity between the amount of attention paid by Helmut Kohl to foreign affairs and that paid by Schröder requires on-going adjustment on the part not only of Germany's allies, but also among career bureaucrats within Germany.

The same situation exists at the parliamentary and grass-roots level. *Bundestag* members from all parties report scant interest among their constituents in security-related topics, although this may change in the wake of 11 September. Bright young politicians no longer see military and security policy as a way to make their names and advance their careers, as was the case during the Cold War.[9] Even among foreign-policy experts in Berlin, there is a strong sense that other foreign-policy issues currently matter more than military and security matters; for example, the issue of EU enlargement, particularly the question of Turkish membership.

Since over two million Turkish citizens live and work in Germany, any questions involving EU relations with Turkey hold special significance for the Federal Republic. Resentment of the US support for Turkish membership of the EU crosses German party lines. 'That is simply not a matter for the US,' says Karl Lamers, foreign-policy spokesman for the opposition CDU. Hans-Ulrich Klose, his counterpart in the SPD, agrees that US pressure on this issue is unwarranted. He suggests that it would be like Germany telling the US to open its border to Mexico completely. Ironically, the United States feels that it is only exerting minimal pressure on Germany over this issue – but Germans clearly perceive even this as undue interference, thereby highlighting the sensitivity of the topic.

There is also the matter of the costs of German unification, which are often treated by other nations as though they were met a long time ago, whereas in fact they continue to run at over DM1bn per year. Comments from Germany's allies that this amount represents only a tiny fraction of the German defence budget, and that it would affect the percentage of German GDP spent on defence only marginally if it were to be included, are unwelcome.

German criticism of American attitudes to Germany is on the increase. While German policy-makers have no doubts that

American military involvement in Europe is essential, they share the widespread European view that the United States is becoming increasingly self-centred, arrogant and erratic. There is a prevailing view that the US in the second Bush era (in contrast to the first) is being driven solely by domestic political concerns, although this view became less critical after the terrorist attacks. Nonetheless, in light of what Germans view as US shirking of certain international responsibilities – via non-ratification of the Comprehensive Test-Ban Treaty (CTBT), or plans to disregard the Anti-Ballistic Missile (ABM) Treaty – American suggestions that Germany might not be fulfilling its security responsibilities rankle.

Sustained Support for Conscription

The defence issue, however, on which German thinking differs most significantly from that in the US, France and the UK is conscription. Policy-makers in Washington, Paris and London often assume that the Berlin government secretly shares their views that conscription has outlived its usefulness, but must publicly tread delicately around this issue for fear of inciting public disapproval. American policy-makers in particular see public opinion as – in the jargon of political science – a dependent variable, and wonder why the German leadership does not make more active efforts to change this variable.

While there are senior German figures, especially among the Greens, who agree with this viewpoint, the majority of policy-makers, practitioners and even academic theorists in Germany consider conscription not only well suited but also essential to facing today's security challenges. To assume that they are paying lip service to it for fear of running foul of public opinion is to miss the point. The problem is not insufficient political will to abolish conscription – the reality is that top German policy-makers see insufficient evidence that this move is necessary.

Both of the dominant political parties in Germany, the SPD and the CDU, support conscription. In both public and private, German policy-makers from a variety of parties and ministries detail numerous firmly held beliefs as to why conscription remains necessary. The reasons are historical in origin – there is a fear that if the military were to become decoupled from German society it could once again pose both a domestic and international threat, as it did twice in the twentieth century.

This view is as pervasive as it is mistaken. Reduced to its

simplest form, it suggests that the professionalisation of a military force increases the risk that such a military will set off on a path of reckless belligerence, without the approval of the civilian leadership. Yet examples abound, both in history and the present day, of professional militaries that remain firmly under civilian control. The heart of the issue is not professionalisation but the maintenance of effective democratic, civilian control of the military; simply to say that the existence of a professional military poses a threat is to misread history. Nonetheless, one fact is indisputable, and that is the weight this view still retains among both policy-makers and the public.

Apart from the historical justification, Germans offer many other reasons for maintaining conscription. According to official pronouncements by the *Bundeswehr*, it ensures the following four necessary conditions:

- that the average intelligence of conscripts remains above an acceptable threshold;
- that a representative cross-spectrum of society is drawn into the military;
- that a large pool of reservists with military experience exists, should the need for mobilisation arise; and
- that the *Bundeswehr* has a ready pool of young talent which it can convince to serve for a longer period of time.

The *Bundeswehr* leadership is in complete agreement with the official line. A senior adviser to the British Defence Minister, Geoffrey Hoon, recalls the impassioned defence of conscription that former Inspector General of the *Bundeswehr* Hans-Peter von Kirchbach would give at classified meetings. Hoon gained the impression that conscription had become a deeply held personal belief for not only Kirchbach but also other senior German military officers.[10] Current Inspector General Harald Kujat shares the views of his predecessor. At the November 2000 *Kommandeurtagung*, or meeting of commanders of the *Bundeswehr*, Kujat strongly defended conscription in response to suggestions made by German President Johannes Rau that a rethink might be needed. Kujat reportedly informed Rau that 'everyone in the room supported conscription', and that, without conscription, 'neither he nor many of the other assembled officers would have joined the army at all'.[11] Understandably, those who have reached the top echelons in a conscription-based system are likely to be loath to change it. For his part, Rudolf Scharping endorsed both Kujat's remarks and the principle of conscription in his own remarks at the meeting.

Scharping is hardly alone among leading German politicians in holding this view. Elected officials across a variety of parties echo *Bundeswehr* statements both on and off the record. Discussions in the Berlin Foreign Ministry with senior civil servants (who, in contrast to the Foreign Ministry's Green leaders, are often supporters of the liberal Free Democratic Party (FDP) or the CDU) include many of the same comments. A senior foreign affairs official has stated that 'one really cannot say that a professional or a conscript army is better'.[12] One senior security adviser to Gerhard Schröder argues that, in light of unification and the absorption of the former NVA, the *Bundeswehr* has been through too many changes in too short a time to tackle the additional issue of professionalisation now.[13] And no less a figure than Richard von Weizsäcker argues that the basic human inability to foresee the future, and the unpredictability of security issues in Europe – the same justification London and Paris use to justify professionalisation – demand that Germany maintain at the very least a core of conscripted forces.[14]

A corollary to these views is the necessity, in the eyes of the current government, to keep open most of the hundreds of small bases scattered around the country. Behind this is the unwillingness of parliamentarians to tolerate closures in their electoral districts, although the official justification is once again given as the necessity of maintaining healthy civil–military relations. But while this is undoubtedly an important task, is maintaining hundreds of small bases the most cost-effective way to achieve it? This question notwithstanding, even Scharping's limited plans for a few base closures (discussed in Chapter Two) prompted strikes by civilian base employees in the spring of 2001.

The above discussion has examined the ways in which German elected officials defend conscription. Popular terms of discussion are even more blunt. In interviewing Scharping, the weekly magazine *Der Spiegel* suggested that, in the absence of a draft, only 'Rambos, rightists and idiots' would go into military service.[15] Similarly, the *Bundeswehrverband,* a soldiers' association, insists that the draft is the only way to maintain a high quality of soldier, because foreign examples show that professional armies can only

Table 2 Conscription in NATO Member States

	Number of Conscripts	Notes
Canada	0	Conscription ended 1945
US	0	Conscription ended July 1973
NATO Europe		
Belgium	0	Conscription ended June 1993
Czech Republic	25,000	
Denmark	5,600	
France	19,150	Conscription ends 2002
Germany	118,400	
Greece	98,320	
Hungary	22,900	
Iceland	n.a.	No military forces
Italy	86,760	Conscription ends 2006
Luxembourg	0	Conscription ended 1967
Netherlands	0	Conscription ended January 1997
Norway	15,200	
Poland	91,600	
Portugal	8,130	
Spain	3,300	Conscription ends 2001
Turkey	391,000	
United Kingdom	0	Conscription ended 1962
Total	**885,360**	

Source: The Military Balance 2001–02 (IISS, October 2001).

recruit 'societally marginal groups'.[16]

Such talk unnecessarily causes tensions with those countries that have professional forces, and more particularly within the circles of professional military officers from Germany's allies who must deal with their German colleagues. However, it does bear remembering that fear of 'marginal groups' – often a euphemism for right-wing extremists – joining an all-volunteer military has a different meaning in the former home of Nazism. Polls indicated in 2001 that youths suspected of having neo-Nazi sympathies (as judged by their membership of fringe right-wing quasi-political parties) disproportionately viewed the *Bundeswehr* as a desirable employer.[17] Any scandal involving behaviour reminiscent of Nazism on the part of soldiers makes national and international headlines. Hence one preceived virtue of conscription is that it prevents an over-representation of this segment within the fighting force. However, a careful process of recruitment and screening could serve the same result, were the *Bundeswehr* willing to make the effort. If the pollsters can identify high-risk youth groups, surely the *Bundeswehr* could as well.

There are, of course, dissenting voices on the issue of conscription, but these remain in the minority. The junior member in the governing coalition, the Green Party, opposes conscription for several reasons. Among them is the potential legal liability created by the scenario of maintaining conscription *de jure*, while *de facto* severely reducing the number of those drafted. This issue is, in fact, one of the few that might force a change of opinion on conscription, were there to be a court challenge.

A legal basis for such a challenge exists. The German Basic Law guarantees *Wehrgerechtigkeit*, a notion that translates roughly as 'defence fairness'. It means that the responsibility for defence should not fall disproportionately upon any particular segment of the population. Because of this, there would be a serious problem if a draftee decided to challenge conscription in the courts. A senior Green foreign-policy figure and one of Joschka Fischer's closest confidantes outlines the following possible scenario: 'One young man has to sit in the mud for a few hundred D-Marks. Meanwhile his classmate, during the same period, starts a booming business. The first young man would be justified in suing, claiming there was no "defence fairness" in this.'

The Greens are not alone in their opinions. As mentioned above, President Johannes Rau has questioned the future of conscription. Six of the nineteen members of a high-calibre independent commission established under the lead of Richard von Weizsäcker to suggest ways to reform the *Bundeswehr* (discussed in Chapter Two) opposed maintaining conscription. There are also dissenting voices in the academic world. Hans-Dieter Lemke, a leading military analyst based at *Stiftung Wissenschaft und Politik* in Ebenhausen, suggests the abolition of conscription on budgetary grounds. While not arguing against conscription *per se*, he points out that the *Bundeswehr* remains chronically underfunded and that ending the costly training of large numbers of conscripts could produce over DM2bn in savings.[18]

These dissenting voices notwithstanding, throughout the debate over how best to plan reform of the German military, there was never any serious doubt about the maintenance of conscription. Even Joschka Fischer decided early in the *Bundeswehr* debate not to offer any serious resistance to the continuance of the draft. The sense among the leadership of the Greens was that there was no hope of their view prevailing, and that they should keep their powder dry, so to speak, for more obtainable goals.

Moreover, even those who did call for an end to conscription admit that such a step would cause social problems unique to Germany, namely a shortfall in social services. The German draft system supplies not one but two forces: the *Bundeswehr* on the one hand and a kind of social welfare army, called the *Zivildienst*, or 'civil service', on the other. This *Zivildienst*, which effectively forms an 'army of helpers' *(Heer der Helfer)*, provides a welcome form of cheap labour to charities by allowing conscientious objectors to work for them instead of the military in a *de facto* national-service programme.

This 'social welfare army' arises, like so much else about the *Bundeswehr*, out of historical considerations. *Bundeswehr* planners, remembering the tragic Nazi era, wanted to ensure that those young Germans who objected to military service in the wake of Nazism could opt out. Hence German conscriptees have the option to choose to register themselves as conscientious objectors, or *'Zivis'* as they are nicknamed in Germany. No small percentage of young men choose this option: in 1999, the last full year before reform planning began, the ratio of those choosing military service to those becoming *Zivis* was nearly one-to-one, with approximately 135,000 carrying out military service, and roughly 124,000 performing alternative service.[19] Nearly two-thirds of the *Zivis* served a 13-month term (reduced on 1 July 2000 to 11 months) in a variety of charitable establishments, such as hospitals and nursing homes. Roughly 100,000 work at the Red Cross, Caritas and Diakonie and other prominent welfare agencies.

Need for this type of labour will only grow as Germany's greying demographics produce a surplus of elderly retired people with few or no children to care for them. Ending the stream of conscripts would mean the end of this 'social army', and as yet no one is entirely sure how to solve this problem. In a time of worldwide economic downturn, replacement labour would be available, but the problem would then be funding the salaries and benefits, which would be greater than those given to conscripts. In short, Germans have a host of social-cohesion concerns and expectations which they believe conscription addresses.

The issue of conscription has particularly caused tension with France, in view of its recent decision to abolish the draft. President Chirac announced in February 1996 that France would professionalise and slim down its armed forces from a strength of approximately half a million troops to an estimated 136,000 men by the year 2002. The army alone was projected to shrink by 100,000.[20] This announcement caught Germany off guard. The decision-making process on this topic was at first kept a closely guarded secret, then moved rapidly towards implementation. Since Germany perceives itself to have a 'special relationship' with France on the issue of defence, being kept in the dark, particularly regarding conscription, caused much resentment. There are some suggestions that French Prime Minister Lionel Jospin had himself been opposed to this slimming down of the military, and had given Germany the impression that the issue was still under debate when in fact this was no longer the case. He did not prepare his German colleagues well for Chirac's announcement; nor did they seem to understand that the president of France (in contrast the largely ceremonial president of Germany) had the last say in this matter.

As a result, the French decision to put an end to conscription with little consultation caused resentment among Germans. Continued French promotion of this decision during the formulation of German military reform plans did little to improve the situation. On the one-year anniversary of the Kosovo engagement, French Defence Minister Alain Richard made a series of speeches praising the results of French force restructuring. On 22 February 2000, he declared that French involvement in Kosovo 'validated the principles of our new defence model', in particular 'total professionalisation'.[21]

Differing Risk Prioritisation

To understand why Germany plans to maintain conscription while its closest European allies, the UK, France and Italy, have decided to abolish it, one must understand not only conscription's domestic political appeal, but also the way in which it assuages German fears regarding international security threats. One of the most significant German justifications for continuing conscription is based upon an international threat assessment that differs from that of its key allies. While commentators in London, Paris and Washington call for German power projection, security analysts in Berlin never stoppped placing traditional homeland defence high, if not first, on their list of priorities. Instability in the former Soviet Union remains a prime security concern among all parties and ministries. Noted peace researcher Harald Müller accurately summarises in public the private views of many policy-makers:

> *From the NATO standpoint ... there is only one serious threat: that of the collapse of the Russian armed forces and the concomitant risk of an unintentional or unauthorized nuclear launch, or of a paranoid reaction to a presumed but non-existent Western attack, brought about by the catastrophic state of the Russian early-warning system.*[22]

These views help to explain the surprisingly warm reception that Russian leader Vladimir Putin has repeatedly received in Germany and the cordiality shown to Gerhard Schröder on a visit to St Petersburg in the spring of 2001. Putin has skilfully used his knowledge of both the German language and American disregard for the ABM Treaty as a means of strengthening Russian relations with the Schröder government. For their part, German leaders, along with those in the UK and France, are adopting a policy of friendliness towards Putin in the hope that this will be a more effective strategy to reform his behaviour than the Bush administration's approach of confrontation.[23] (Scharping found himself caught in some of the cross-currents of this tricky relationship when, during a visit to Moscow in January 2001, he reportedly sympathised with Russian concerns about America's missile defence plans – only to see Schröder voice new willingness to work with the US on missile defence a month later.[24])

Meanwhile, Germany's allies have a raft of different priorities, ranging from the fight against terrorism to the not strictly military challenges posed by drug smuggling, illegal immigration and a host of other types of organised crime that threaten public order and stability. But whereas territorial defence had dramatically retreated in the mindset of London and Paris, it remained at the forefront of security planning in Berlin. The reason for this can once again be found in the historical character of the *Bundeswehr* as a territorial defence force. Downplaying the role of home defence would mean downplaying justification for the *Bundeswehr* itself. And since members of an institution rarely enjoy downplaying the justification for their own existence, they try to avoid it whenever possible.

In addition, German military professionals are very reticent (in contrast to their French or British counterparts) about the notion of force projection worldwide. For example, the desire of Foreign Minister Fischer for involvement in East Timor met with great resistance among the professionals in the German Defence Ministry who were faced with actually executing the deployment. Fischer's efforts to challenge the military consensus on this issue were seriously undercut by the lack of a German capability for force projection. This issue only became more problematic after NATO invoked Article V in September 2001.

Summary

This chapter has outlined the distinctive characteristics that define German military reform. First, there is a lack of urgency regarding the pace and timing of military reform, due largely to Germany's perception that its strategic position has improved greatly since the end of the Cold War. Another key characteristic is the limited high-level interest in this topic. Unlike President Bush or Prime Minister Blair, before 11 September, Chancellor Schröder did not place security and defence issues at the top of his personal priority list. The issue played little or no role in either national or local elections, which were instead dominated by concerns about immigration, pensions and declining benefits. Moreover, senior German leaders of all parties (except the Greens) see no reason to drop conscription, even though the trend within NATO is clearly towards doing so. Finally, instability in Russia remains the main German strategic concern. These characteristics are of more than sociological or historical interest. They have determined the decision-making process that drives *Bundeswehr* reform. As the next chapter will describe, Schröder's cabinet and particularly Defence Minister Scharping faced a variety of proposals in 2000 and 2001 as to how best to reform the *Bundeswehr*. The historical and social context described here shaped the choices that they made. Instead of picking various 'fast-track' options towards modernisation, or increasing defence spending to pay for reform, German leaders opted for as much continuity as possible, in particular the continued downgrading of the amount of budget allocated to defence. As a result, the 'new *Bundeswehr'* will, in fact, look very much like the old.

Chapter 2

The Content of *Bundeswehr* Reform

Although *Bundeswehr* reform made headlines in 2001, in a broader sense it had been going on for more than a decade. Throughout the 1990s, CDU-led governments concentrated on the slow process of creating political tolerance for German military involvement outside of NATO territories. However, the CDU lost power in the election of autumn 1998. The centre-left SPD received a larger plurality (40.9%) than it had originally expected in the national vote. Rather than entering into a 'grand coalition' with the CDU, as it appears both Schröder and the voters expected would happen, the SPD instead found itself in a strong enough position to call upon the Greens, who obtained 6.7% of the vote, to serve as junior coalition partner.

Traditionally in German politics, the junior party receives the Foreign Ministry, but there was some speculation as to whether the highly non-traditional Green Party would prefer other posts. Moreover, the SPD's former (unsuccessful) candidate for the chancellery, Rudolf Scharping, showed clear interest in serving as foreign minister. Nonetheless, the *de facto* leader of the Greens, Joschka Fischer, chose to follow tradition and become head of the German Foreign Ministry. Over at the Chancellery, the career diplomat and Balkan expert Michael Steiner became Schröder's top foreign and security policy adviser. Steiner's influence on foreign policy increased steadily throughout 2000 and into 2001, until he was blamed for the May 2001 scandal over the leak of a secret memo of a conversation between Schröder and President Bush. He was not forced to resign but the episode dimmed his lustre.[1]

Having lost the chance to shape foreign policy to Fischer and Steiner, Scharping reluctantly became minister of defence instead and began navigating the tricky waters of defence diplomacy. Some observers speculated that Scharping, who still hopes to become chancellor, comforted himself by remembering that Helmut Schmidt advanced from the Defence Ministry to the Chancellery when Willy Brandt resigned in 1974.

One of the first acts of the new red–green coalition was, in October 1998, to call for a two-year assessment of the future needs of the *Bundeswehr*. The object of this move was to buy the new government time in its consideration of defence issues while it began planning for what it viewed as more pressing issues – tax and pension reform. On top of these projects, once Hans Eichel became finance minister (after Oskar Lafontaine's brief tenure in that post), Germany advanced on a strict budget-cutting course. Eichel's goal is to eradicate, by 2006, the need for Germany to take on any new debt.[2] When Eichel came on board, his enthusiasm for significant budget-cutting worried Scharping. Consequently, the Defence Minister decided to move the reform-planning timescale forward in the hope of better defending his portion of the budget.[3]

Hence the 'two-year review', which did not get under way until 1999, was shortened, with the resulting reports all appearing in the spring of 2000. One report came from a high-calibre commission under the leadership of the former president, Richard von Weizsäcker; a second arose from an internal defence ministry review under the leadership of then Inspector General Hans-Peter von Kirchbach; the third and ultimately most decisive report was Scharping's own assessment, which was very similar to the Kirchbach report (excerpts appear in the Appendix).

Three Reform Proposals: The Weizsäcker, Kirchbach and Scharping Reports

Exactly why three separate reports emerged has been a subject of much speculation. There are three plausible versions as to how it came about. The first version focuses on Scharping's personal ambitions. Senior officials involved in the reform process suggest that during the first year of his tenure at the Defence Ministry, Scharping's mind was rather more on his own career moves than on his ministry.[4] At the time, before the CDU imploded due to a party-finance corruption scandal, there was widespread speculation about a potential collapse of Schröder's red–green government. Its replacement would presumably have been the grand coalition of the CDU and SPD that had been expected during the 1998 election – but with Scharping in some kind of senior role, presumably foreign minister, and without Schröder and Steiner. However, the collapse of the CDU in late 1999 and early 2000 quashed such speculation and ended both the CDU's, and Scharping's, ambitions of overtaking Schröder before the next election. Scharping finally began to concentrate fully on *Bundeswehr* reform, perhaps as an alternate way of advancing his rivalry with Schröder. At this point he realised that the early outlines of the initial report, that of the Weizsäcker Commission, were already clear – and were too radical for him. He therefore instructed Kirchbach to prepare an official Defence Ministry proposal on the same topic, which presumably would be more realistic. However, this report emerged as too conservative. Scharping would ultimately accept Kirchbach's resignation as well as his report. As a result, this hypothesis goes, Scharping had no alternative other than to write a report himself.

A second version of events suggests that Scharping intended to play Weizsäcker and Kirchbach off against one another all along, so that he could appear as the man of the centre by choosing a middle course between them. However, a third version is more charitable towards Scharping and his multiple commissions. Proponents of this version say that Scharping's attention to his job never wavered; nor did he ever intend to play the reports off against each other, or use reform as a potential stick with which to beat Schröder. Rather, Scharping simply wanted as much input as possible into a difficult and complex process, one which was originally scheduled to play out over a much longer time period than became the case. It is difficult to ascertain with absolute certainty which of these three versions is most accurate; most probably, aspects of all three versions have merit.

There was also much speculation and amazement at the alacrity with which Scharping moved from the release of these reports to a cabinet vote. Both the Weizsäcker and Kirchbach reports were presented to the public on 23 May 2000, with Scharping's own version following at the end of the same month. Despite the complexity of the topic involved, Scharping saw to it that the cabinet approved his plans on 14 June, in time for the 21 June decision on the budget for 2001. The brief period of time between the presentation of the proposals and cabinet approval drew much criticism from politicians in the coalition governing parties, the opposition and the media. The suggestion was that Scharping was trying to stifle opposing voices (and protect himself from attack by cabinet colleagues) by rushing through a decision on the matter before the summer parliamentary holidays.[5]

Although Scharping's own proposals are the ones that will guide implementation, it is nonetheless worthwhile to examine all three of the reports that he commissioned. Taken together, these three reports reveal both the spectrum of German policy opinion and the limits of its tolerance.

The 'Missed Opportunity' of the Weizsäcker Commission Report

The Weizsäcker report initially received the most public attention because a series of leaks throughout May 2000 suggested that it would offer a vision for radical restructuring. It is worth examining in detail because increasing numbers of German and foreign leaders currently see it as a significant 'missed opportunity'. There is a growing sense among German policy-makers that its suggestions, which were indeed radical by German standards, deserve a serious second look.

What does this 'missed-opportunity' report say? Its tone is very blunt. It describes the *Bundeswehr* as 'too big, ill-composed, and increasingly out of step with the times'. Moreover, '[t]he *Bundeswehr* has no future in its current structure. The present form of military service produces a surplus of manpower altogether, but a shortage of operational forces. Outdated materiel diminishes its operational capability and causes operating costs to soar. The current budget estimates allow no scope for adequate modernisation under the present structure and form of military service.[6]'

The report states that 'the yardstick for the new *Bundeswehr* should be the capability to participate in up to two crisis response operations simultaneously and indefinitely'. To meet this challenge, the Commission argues that the army needs two brigade-sized operational contingents with the requisite support and command elements; the air force requires two operational contingents with a total of 90–100 combat aircraft, ten ground-based air defence squadrons and aerial refuelling and lift capabilities; and the navy similarly needs two operational contingents capable of conducting joint warfare operations.[7]

In addition, there would have to be an 'operational force component of 140,000 troops that is functional and fit for employment in an alliance role'.[8] Senior Commission member Theo Sommer found it necessary to emphasise at the press conference presenting the report that these 140,000 troops were 'not an intervention army'.[9] Overall, the report argues that the *Bundeswehr* in peacetime should be reduced from its year 2000 size of 323,000 soldiers to 240,000. It recommends reducing civil posts to around 80,000, and streamlining command structures and increasing the authority of the Inspector General. It also calls for an annual increase in the *Bundeswehr*'s budget of roughly DM2–3bn, saying 'you have to spend to save'. It even leans in the direction of the French by emphasising the need to develop a capacity for Europe to act 'without American co-operation'.[10]

Notably, even the 'radical' Weizsäcker Commission report viewed conscription as a continuing necessity. Although six of the nineteen members opposed maintaining conscription, the majority of the commissioners agreed with the prevailing assumptions regarding its continuation. The report recommends that 30,000 conscripts be drawn in annually, providing the core of a reserve.

Overall, in the Commission's view, the 240,000-strong *Bundeswehr* should comprise 210,000 professionals, 25,000 conscripts and 5,000 conscripts who volunteer to serve a longer term.[11] The Commission's report also cites, as a reason to continue the draft, its usefulness as a recruitment tool.[12] However, the report comes up with no clear-cut solution for the violation of *Wehrgerechtigkeit* (or 'defence fairness') that this would cause. It suggests the broad interpretation that a *de facto* partial draft would be fair because it would deprive of their liberty only those men who were actually needed. The report also ducks the question of how to replace the conscientious objectors, or *Zivis*.[13]

Nonetheless, the Commission's view is clear: a *Bundeswehr* that successfully maintains conscription, while simultaneously increasing its deployability, would offer a 'substantial advantage' over a *Bundeswehr* without conscripts, because it would still have sufficient flexibility to face the 'risks of an uncertain future'.[14] Weizsäcker particularly emphasised this point in his remarks at the press conference following the report's release. This argument is the aspect of the Weizsäcker report – which, it must be remembered, is the most radical to emerge from Germany – that is most at variance with British, French and American thinking. These countries perceive the same problem, namely the need for flexibility in the face of risks, and conclude that the best way to face this issue is by training and equipping a slimmed-down professional army. The Commission recognises the same problem, but comes to the opposite conclusion. It sees this as a reason to maintain conscription and thereby also numerical strength.

The Commission's report may be radical by German standards, but it is not radical by, say, American standards. Its conservatism becomes less surprising when one surveys the list of over 100 experts summoned to give formal testimony before the Commission. Only two are foreigners (Wesley Clark of the United States and François Heisbourg of France). While Commission members did consult privately and in small groups with their colleagues abroad, clearly domestic analysis dominated the work of the group as a whole.

Moreover, the report's discussion of the potential threats to German security – which exists only in the full-length German language report, and not in the English-language summary – exhibits the type of risk prioritisation described in chapter one of this paper. Admittedly, the Weizsäcker report does contain the same concerns that are present in the threat assessments of other leading NATO countries, such as concern about weapons of mass destruction and about non-traditional threats such as environmental or information-technology dangers.

What is different is the prioritisation. The full report repeats the order of priorities set by the German government in 1992, whereby territorial defence of the German homeland must come first.[15] While the Weizsäcker report acknowledges the strategic changes since the end of the Cold War, its assessment of the tasks facing German security policy nonetheless begins with a reminder that 'any realistic security policy must take account of the threat of an on-going military threat to the Atlantic Alliance and thereby to Germany' – in other words, collective defence.[16] Such language can hardly be criticised; a nation obviously needs to provide for its own defence. But it is more than mildly surprising to outsiders to find the prioritisation uninflected by an updated view of preventing and containing crises and terrorism abroad as a way of ensuring security at home.

Von Kirchbach's Report and Resignation

Although the Weizsäcker and Kirchbach reports are sometimes contrasted as polar opposites, they do in fact exhibit some similarities. In the German-language version, Kirchbach's substantive proposals, which are also the official proposals of the German Defence Ministry, begin with a section on the 'constitutive framework' of the *Bundeswehr*'s mission. Like the Weizsäcker commission, the Kirchbach report names territorial defence first. 'The basic task of German fighting forces is, as laid down in Article 87a of the Basic Law, territorial defence.'[17] This is obviously an uncontroversial statement, and its appearance in the report is to be expected. Elsewhere in the report, Kirchbach does emphasise the need for crisis prevention and management and increased deployability with an eye towards increasing German capacity to provide both. What is notable is that Kirchbach, in contrast to Scharping in his proposals (to be discussed below), chose to place this reference at the front of the report. He begins his constitutive framework by emphasising territorial defence, and then cites Germany's obligations to its allies. However, neither the Kirchbach nor Scharping reports contain the same kind of explicit acknowledgement of the need to participate in crisis-management outside of the Euro-Atlantic area, as the Strategic Defence Review in the United Kingdom does.[18]

As to the role of conscription, Kirchbach has no doubts about its importance. 'Qualitatively and quantitatively,' he asserts, the only way for the *Bundeswehr* to fulfil its obligations 'is via general conscription and ensuring one has the ability to call up reserves'.[19] Notably, the report declines to reclassify terrorism as a security challenge meriting *Bundeswehr* response, citing the prevalent German view that 'defence against cross-border terrorist activities and organised crime remains, in Germany, a task for the police'.[20]

The specifics of the report have a much more business-as-usual approach to the future of the *Bundeswehr* than the Weizsäcker proposals. Kirchbach was not willing to reduce the overall size of the military as severely; his report calls for an active force strength of approximately 290,000. Of these, roughly 85,000 should be conscripts. The report urges that there should be an operationally deployable force of 157,000. Mechanised divisions should be reduced from a total of seven to five, with an overall emphasis on producing lighter, more deployable forces.

Scharping chose to follow these recommendations more closely than those of the Weizsäcker Commission. Why, then, did Scharping *de facto* dismiss Kirchbach (by choosing to accept his resignation) just one day after Kirchbach submitted his report? In the view of one Foreign Ministry official it was because he was aiming to distract press attention from the fact that he was 'rubbishing' both reports, even though he had actually commissioned them. The official also noted that there had long been poor personal relations between Scharping, a leader of the SPD, and Kirchbach, a holdover from the CDU days. Kirchbach had inspired considerable respect among the troops and the public at large as the 'hero of the Oder'. This title was a reference to his success in the summer of 1997, when he organised *Bundeswehr* relief for an area threatened by flooding from the Oder River. However, Kirchbach was not known for his skill in manoeuvring among top political élites, an ability that General Kujat possesses in ample measure.[21]

Scharping's Own Proposals

The change of personnel at the top notwithstanding, Kirchbach's lingering influence made its presence felt in Scharping's own proposals. These became the official ones, approved by the German government in June 2000. In contrast to Kirchbach's report, billed as coming 'from the ministry', Scharping's proposals are contained in a report identified on its cover page as coming 'from the minister'. This discrepancy, while minor, symbolises the tension between the minister and his staff.

One significant difference in tone between the 'ministry's' and the 'minister's' reports is the prioritisation of the tasks facing the *Bundeswehr*. Showing greater recognition of current foreign-policy imperatives, the Scharping report begins not with an emphasis on territorial defence but with a reiteration of Germany's commitment to its allied obligations. The foreign minister's proposal cites the German Basic Law, but (in contrast to Kirchbach) employs it to make the point that it 'puts Germany under the obligation to serve world peace as an equal part of a united Europe'. However, Scharping does also emphasise that the basic task of the *Bundeswehr* is territorial defence.[22]

The Scharping report also stresses the need to maintain conscription. Like the Weizsäcker and Kirchbach reports, it uses the unpredictability of the future as a justification for conscription. Territorial defence remains a high priority for this reason, because it shields Germany against 'negative developments in the security situation that are currently unlikely but cannot be ruled out'.[23] Security in the face of such uncertainty is only possible, in his opinion, via conscription. On top of this, the 'integration of soldiers in society as citizens' remains a fundamental guiding principle for the *Bundeswehr*.

This assertion has drawn criticism from foreign observers. They complain that Scharping did not do enough to promote the need for professionalisation. They suggest that he should have used the EU's new plans to develop its own autonomous capacity as a means of justifying the abolition of conscription and other radical changes to the German public.

This criticism misses the point. Scharping did try to use the EU's plans as a lever for forcing movement on some reform issues. A public relations effort in late March and early April 2000 included a series of newspaper and radio interviews in which he emphasised that the *Bundeswehr* was no longer capable of fulfilling its commitments to its allies (a lament that would be repeated often in 2001 as well). He particularly regretted deficits in communication, transport and high technology. In his opinion, there was an 'investment deficit' of DM15bn.[24] Scharping had an article published under his name in *Die Zeit* where he said explicitly that 'today, the problem is not that we have too much Americanness but rather too little Europeanness in the responsibility for common security'.[25] He agreed in an interview with the *Frankfurter Allgemeine Zeitung* that American criticisms about the deficits in German capabilities were justified and demanded an answer.[26]

However, where foreign observers projected their own assumptions on to the German Defence Minister is in assuming that he would use these commitments to convince the public of the need for professionalisation. At an early stage in the current reform debate, Scharping, in September 1999 remarks to the *Führungsakademie* (Leadership Academy) of the *Bundeswehr*, made clear that he was against significant decreases in the number of conscripts as a part of *Bundeswehr* reform. Foreign security analysts therefore criticise Scharping for failing to do something – namely win over public sentiment for professionalisation – that he did not in fact attempt to do at all.

On the specifics, Scharping's original proposal suggests a modified version of Kirchbach's numbers. It calls for the overall size of the *Bundeswehr* to be approximately 255,000 soldiers, with 80–90,000 civilian support personnel.[27] (As will be discussed below, Scharping would subsequently raise this total to 285,000.) For the year 2002, Scharping's report calls for a reduction in the term of service to nine months.[28] He also proposes that even this abbreviated term could be interrupted and served non-continuously (see the excerpts from Scharping's report in the Appendix). Starting in 2001, women received the right to participate fully in any *Bundeswehr* capacity. The impact of a reduction in the number of *Zivis* on the social-welfare economy is not discussed, thus leaving a significant hole.

Troubling Questions of Financing

Scharping's report is also vague on the financing of reform. It omits claims (such as those made in the Weizsäcker report) that increases in funding are absolutely necessary; nor does it contain any kind of detailed budget breakdown or spreadsheet for the future. Given the June 2000 decision by the cabinet to approve Finance Minister Hans Eichel's planned decrease in the Defence Ministry budget, and the June 2001 decision to hold to that course with only minor adjustments, this is an unfortunate omission. The military budget, cut by 3.6% to DM45.3bn, was originally planned to drop to DM43.7bn by the year 2003 (although these figures do not include an extra DM2bn that the German Defence Ministry received for costs related to Kosovo).[29] On 30 May 2001, Eichel gave in to pressure from Scharping to increase these amounts somewhat. He granted the Defence Ministry an additional DM500m per year for the years 2003–06. However, the small size of the increase, and the fact that it is not payable until after the next election, meant that the reaction from the German Defence Ministry was less than jubilant.[30] And the overall trend remained the same: defence budgets would decrease for the foreseeable future.

These decreases happened despite Scharping's 1998 insistence that he would only accept the post of defence minister in the first place if the budget were to rise continually to about DM49bn in 2002. Instead, since 1990, the German defence budget has been reduced by over 25% in real terms.[31] In contrast, London and Washington are increasing spending.[32]

To counter criticism, Scharping made many comments to the media in 2000 and 2001 about how the *Bundeswehr* would save by learning to work more efficiently and contracting out to private firms where possible. He convinced over 300 firms to sign an agreement (a *Rahmenvertrag*) promising close cooperation with the *Bundeswehr* in finding ways to save money via contracting out and leasing services and equipment. The Finance Ministry has agreed that the money saved via improved efficiency will stay with the Defence Ministry (rather than reverting to the overall federal budget). Scharping will also be allowed to keep proceeds from sales of assets, up to a ceiling of DM1.2bn, although the *Bundeswehr* was trying to get that amount increased.

When Scharping announced the funds that he expects such measures to yield during a speech to the American Institute of Contemporary German Studies in Washington, he amazed his American listeners. Scharping claimed that he would actually be able to *increase* defence spending by 3.2% in 2001. Members of the Washington policy-making audience were sceptical. The German government takes on new debt totalling 10% of its entire budget every year, while Eichel remains determined to cut costs across the board; defence budget increases would therefore appear highly unlikely. However, a spokesman for the Defence Ministry, when asked for clarification, confirmed that Scharping had been referring to the expected savings to be gleaned from a more efficient operation of the *Bundeswehr*, increased public–private sector cooperation and outsourcing.[33] Scharping himself repeated again to reporters in June 2001 that he expected to release a further DM3bn through savings, increased efficiency and sales of assets.[34]

The specifics of how this will be achieved and the savings the Ministry might reasonably expect in the future remain unclear. Numerous closed-door meetings between Scharping and senior *Bundeswehr* officers in 2000 and 2001 failed to allay the fears of the officers that 'neither the money needed to finance reforms nor the will to insist upon procuring it from the government was there'.[35] A former Inspector General, Admiral Dieter Wellershoff, found Scharping's plans to be very weak, a mixture of 'light and shadows'.[36]

A hard look at the numbers shows that the Defence Ministry will face both short-term and long-term financing problems. In the short term, it became apparent in March 2001 that the *Bundeswehr* was facing a deficit in the current budget of over DM300m, with the army lacking DM110m and the air force DM218m. The Defence Minister announced that the *Bundeswehr* might have to reduce both its readiness and its commitments to NATO.[37] Inspector General Kujat remarked publicly that German forces could no longer be considered fully operational.[38] Eichel's concession on 30 May 2001 to increase the budget starting in 2003 did not provide enough money, or provide it soon enough, to solve this problem.

The long-term picture is similarly troubling. A detailed financial analysis, drawn up by Hans-Dieter Lemke, casts significant doubt on the ability of the *Bundeswehr* to fund its plans under current budget constraints. Lemke has shown that Scharping cannot create the force structure he has proposed within his allotted budget. The target completion date for the bulk of the reform is the year 2006, which represents the end of the next legislative period in Germany. Lemke's assessment, published in late 2000, is of necessity speculative. However, working with the most optimistic possible assumptions – such as assuming a reasonable rate of inflation, no further decreases in military spending, no unexpected major expenditures, and so forth – Lemke estimates a gap of at least DM2.2bn between what the Defence Ministry hopes to implement and what it can afford. The gap could also potentially be much larger, he warns.[39]

Internal *Bundeswehr* estimates appear to be even more pessimistic. Confidential planning papers, leaked to the press at the end of May and beginning of June 2001, predicted funding shortfalls of billions of D-marks. One source predicted a DM20bn shortfall for the entire reform process.[40] Meanwhile, *Die Zeit* cited Inspector General Kujat as saying that he lacked DM2.6bn for the 2002 budget. On top of this, Kujat needed another DM220bn, or DM15bn annually until 2015, for necessary procurement.[41]

Questions about how the Defence Ministry would afford two of its costliest desiderata – satellites and transport aircraft – became the focus of public scrutiny in the spring and summer of 2001. In

October 2000 Scharping confirmed his desire to acquire four to six radar satellites and 73 transport aircraft, omitting to clarify either then or later how they would be paid for.[42] Former Defence Minister Volker Rühe, together with his French colleague François Léotard, wrote an article for the *Frankfurter Allgemeine Zeitung* decrying the fact that *neither* of these projects had clear financing.[43] Despite these problems, Chancellor Schröder assured his NATO allies at the Brussels summit in June 2001 that Germany's decision to acquire the 73 Airbus transport planes was final. Germany in fact signed a Memorandum of Understanding (MOU) committing to this purchase at the Paris Air Show later that month. These acquisition plans prompted further sceptical commentary in the press, given the on-going lack of financing.[44] Meanwhile, press reports circulated comments from both the Inspector General and ordinary soldiers about the poor state of *Bundeswehr* morale, after years of underfunding and with no relief in sight.[45]

Reform Implementation

Despite these troubling questions of finance, the Defence Ministry began moving forward with implementation in 2001. Inspector General Kujat was charged with outlining the next steps. Under his guidance, the German Defence Ministry prepared an overview, or *Grobausplanung,* of how it would implement the guidelines laid out in Scharping's proposals. It presented this overview (from which excerpts appear in the Appendix) to Scharping at the end of September 2000. Shortly thereafter, the Ministry also made public both the overview and a subsequent intermediate summary, or *Zwischenbilanz.*[46] A third follow-up document on specifics, known as the *Feinausplanung,* was published at the end of January 2001. The *Zwischenbilanz* and the *Feinausplanung* do not make any dramatic challenges to the guidelines established by Scharping, but do alter some of the numbers. They establish the following target numbers:

- 255,000 active troops (including 80,000 conscripts);
- 22,000 non-active troops undergoing long-term professional training;
- 5,000 reservists undergoing full-time service;
- 282,000 total as target.

It should be noted that the detailed plan of January 2001 modified the total slightly, calling for a target of 285,000 overall, but did not provide information on the additional 3,000 troops.

These numbers reflect the belief prevalent in Berlin that 250,000 is a kind of 'magic number'. Below this strength, the maintenance of costly elements of the infrastructure – such as academies and exercise ranges – ceases to make sense. Painful political questions about base and institution closures would then arise. It is precisely these kinds of deep cuts, however, that the *Bundeswehr* needs to make if it is to stay within its budget limits and reform.

The *Zwischenbilanz* focuses not on cutbacks but on promised improvements. In particular, it emphasises that working conditions will be made more attractive for conscripts.[47] The target numbers for conscripts are as follows:

- 26,500 conscripts serving an interrupted service of six months followed by three months at a later date;
- 26,500 conscripts serving for nine continuous months;
- 27,000 conscripts who voluntarily extend their time of service up to 23 months.[48]

The previous distinction between a main defence force and a crisis reaction force will be dropped. Instead, there will be a pool of deployable forces of 150,000 soldiers.[49] The Defence Ministry considers this an appropriate size for fulfilling Germany's NATO and EU commitments. These deployable forces will be supported by 108,000 troops in the military *Grundorganisation*, or basic organisation. The army, air force and navy will transfer men to a strengthened medical service and a new service branch, a *Streitkräftebasis* or fighting-force support service (sometimes translated as Joint Support Service).[50] Outlines for the division of personnel among these services (available on the *Bundeswehr* web site, www.bundeswehr.de) are: army, 138,500 troops; air force, 51,850; *Streitkräftebasis*, an estimated 50,000; navy, approximately 22,600. (One must cite these numbers with caution, since figures quoted by the *Bundeswehr* sometimes exclude the troops from the respective services serving with the Medical Services and the Joint Support Service.)

Despite statements to the contrary in 2000, in early 2001 Scharping announced that *Bundeswehr* reform would also include some base closures. Although there was some uncertainty over the exact number and which bases would come under the axe, by the end of February 2001 the Defence Ministry appeared prepared to do the following: close 38 large and 20 small bases, while keeping open 463 other bases. The estimated savings produced by these closures would be approximately DM200m.

Even these relatively limited cuts touched off a storm of protest, partly because of the parochial concerns of parliamentarians, and partly because of the historical desire to bind the military closely to local society through widely scattered emplacements. Bavarian politicians were particularly angered by plans for base closures in their state, where the SPD did not do well electorally. The General Secretary of the CSU accused Scharping of political motives.[51] Base workers themselves protested via strikes in the spring of 2001.

Another reform was a change in the venerable *Blankeneser Erlass*, a decree from the time of Chancellor Helmut Schmidt that divided authority among the Inspector General and his subordinates. This division had long been criticised as unworkable in the event of a serious crisis. The *Erlass* was modified to give increased powers to the Inspector General.

As for the role of women, female applicants will henceforth be eligible to participate in all aspects of the *Bundeswehr*, although there are no plans to conscript them. To enable full participation for women in the *Bundeswehr*, the *Bundestag* approved necessary changes to the Basic Law at the end of October 2000.[52] At the time of writing, over 1,221 women had voluntarily applied for positions in the *Bundeswehr* and 138 had been accepted.[53] In addition to improvements in pay, both conscripts and those serving voluntarily will also have expanded opportunities to learn skills for later civilian employment.[54]

In fact, cooperation with private industry is one of the key components of the way reform is emerging. A new private firm was formed to help the *Bundeswehr* to function in a more cost-effective manner. This office, known by its German initials GEBB (*Gesellschaft für Entwicklung, Beschaffung und Betrieb*), in conjunction with six banks, will manage *Bundeswehr* properties that could also have commercial uses.[55]

Obviously the willingness of private industry to lend its expertise in aid of *Bundeswehr* reform does not arise from altruism.

With *Bundeswehr* restructuring will come new procurement decisions, and a variety of (primarily European) firms stand to benefit. The overview and *Zwischenbilanz* make clear that the Defence Ministry prioritises air transport, intelligence-gathering and improved command and interoperability. Numerous improvements in IT capabilities are also planned.

The Arms Industry and German Procurement

Given the purchasing intentions of the *Bundeswehr*, what does the course of *Bundeswehr* reform imply for procurement? Is there a clear trend in procurement emerging? To answer these questions, it is first necessary to review briefly the development of the international arms industry in 1999–2001. The issue of who purchases what, where and from whom is always tricky, but it became even more complex with the creation of the European Aeronautic, Defence and Space Company (EADS) via a combination primarily of Daimler Chrysler Aerospace (Dasa) and Aerospatiale Matra.[56] This company, which formally came into being on 10 July 2000, controls 80% of the Airbus consortium. It has a combined annual revenue of roughly $22bn, making it the world's third largest defence company behind Boeing ($55bn) and Lockheed Martin ($28bn).[57]

The creation of EADS coincided with a period of reassessment on both sides of the Atlantic of the future of military procurement. In Europe, Hanns Maull has called for the 'creation of a common European approach to procurement, with far-reaching supranational authority'.[58] European defence ministers exhibited this spirit at the Farnborough Air Show in July 2000. The defence ministers of Germany, the UK, France, Italy, Spain and Sweden signed an agreement or 'letter of intent' (LOI) regarding common rules on arms policy, export research, definition of needs and industrial and technological security.[59] The trend continued with the signing of the MOU for the purchase of transport aircraft at the Paris Air Show of July 2001 (more on this topic below).

On the other side of the Atlantic, American defence experts are critical of the European desire to reinvent various defence wheels at great cost. In the words of John Deutch, Arnold Kanter and Brent Scowcroft, 'Europe is building a separate "European" defence industry, based in part on short-sighted, if not downright misguided, calculations of self-interest'. As they see it, 'our European allies have been producing their own hardware – even when it is more costly and less advanced than what they could buy from the United States'.[60] The prime example of this in their view is the Eurofighter.

However, they go on to admit that one of the main incentives for Europeans to build a separate industry is the US unwillingness to open its own markets and remove barriers to the exchange of information. The authors find the US habit of giving security classifications to equipment and technology justified when it is intended to protect troops, but not when its purpose is to serve as *de facto* economic protectionism. As a solution, Deutch, Kanter and Scowcroft call for an increase in the opportunities and incentives for transatlantic mergers and cooperation, particularly at the second-tier level of suppliers.

Some US initiatives notwithstanding, a Pentagon spokesman agrees that there is an enormous 'level playing field' problem.[61] Europeans complain that they are expected to buy American products while the US does not buy European. However, the Pentagon views the output of the European defence industry as emblematic of the problems of state-owned and subsidised industries: they create products that are neither as good nor as cheap as those manufactured by American companies subject to market forces.

More cynical commentators speculate that the progress that has been made in the last couple of years on ESDP is, in fact, purely industry-driven. One American analyst says that the weaknesses of the European defence industry are greatly exaggerated, given the success enjoyed by Airbus. European commentators are united in asserting that this hypothesis is nonsense, and 'the pot calling the kettle black' to boot.

How do these issues intersect with *Bundeswehr* reform? Reform does reveal one clear trend in procurement intentions: German policy-makers see a compelling political imperative to give precedence to European procurement. Two major procurement decisions solidified this preference: decisions on strategic lift and on intelligence gathering. The *Bundeswehr* became acutely aware of its lack of ability to deploy troops by air, not only in Kosovo, but also in smaller-scale situations such as the sending of humanitarian aid to Turkey after the 1999 earthquake. Germany had to rent an Antonov aircraft to provide lift, and had to convince the private firm BASF to lend its own corporate fire-rescue squad for the deployment.[62]

The need for an aircraft with the capacity to move very heavy cargoes, along the lines of a US C-17, to replace the Transall, has long been on the minds of German decision-makers. Germany is also part of the FLA (Future Large Aircraft) group, a European working group dedicated to assessing the options for future procurement. For the Germans, purchasing such lift capability in America is viewed as politically inappropriate. The only real question in 2000 was whether Germany would choose the Ukrainian Antonov-70, in a kind of political trade-off for cooperation on Chernobyl, or whether it would bow to French pressure to purchase the Airbus A-400M. The inclination among defence circles was towards France, but there were obvious political advantages in keeping the Ukrainian option open as long as possible. However, the announcement of the British decision to go with Airbus, combined with Chirac's visit to Germany and the Franco-German summit in June 2000, tipped the balance. By July 2000, at the Farnborough Air Show in Great Britain, defence ministers from Germany, France, Spain, the UK, Italy, Belgium and Turkey were ready to announce publicly their intention to procure a total of 225 A-400Ms (although that number was later revised downwards to 212). Germany signalled an intent to order the largest consignment, a total of 73, for an undisclosed price. And in June 2001, Germany became one of seven states to sign the MOU committing to these purchases, despite the fact that financing for it remained unresolved. A report in *Die Zeit* speculated that there was some kind of deal that Germany would pay the full amount on delivery in 2006–08 – thereby making the whole issue some future government's problem.[63]

The size of the potential German order has surprised many analysts. Indeed, it is three times that agreed by the United Kingdom. Suspicion abounded that the real objective was to secure construction jobs for Germany rather than a real German capability. In other words, given the sinking German defence budget, British commentators wondered whether declaring an intent to procure a large number of aircraft was actually a bid 'to wrest a greater share of the industrial cake from its partners, or even an attempt to take the wing-design leadership'.[64] Whatever the motivation, this procurement decision gave an important shot in the arm to Airbus.

Understanding the resentments and friction between Germany and the United States also helps to explain another procurement decision that surprised not only Americans but also the British. The French had long been pushing for development of an independent satellite intelligence-gathering capability; this desire received new impetus, in French eyes, from the American reluctance to share information during the Gulf War. However, in light of all the other shortfalls in EU defence spending, London has been less concerned about the need to develop a separate European satellite capability at great cost when one might use existing NATO capabilities.

Germany has come down on the French side, after experiencing frustrations of its own during the Kosovo conflict, due to fact that the US would only allow it to play a minor role in the selection of targets. There had at one point been early efforts at Franco-German collaboration on satellite issues. A former senior adviser to Volker Rühe, Ulrich Weisser, particularly laments the decision of Helmut Kohl to drop plans to develop both optical and radar satellites with the French in the mid-1990s. Saying this was due to lack of funds 'was hard to believe', in his view. 'The result of this damaged our trustworthiness in the eyes of France and damaged the European – above all the German – industry, and caused a delay in the creation of an important element of the European ability to act.'[65] The French decided to proceed with the project themselves, despite the high cost (about $2m per satellite, with high operational costs).[66]

In June 2000, Gerhard Schröder essentially reversed Kohl's earlier decision. At a bilateral Franco-German summit on June 2000 in Mainz, the two leaders announced that Germany would cooperate with France in producing an independent satellite observation system. France will contribute its optical satellite, the *Helios* II, while Germany will contribute the all-weather radar satellite (SAR-LUPE).[67] Germany expects to spend approximately DM600m over several years.[68]

Yet another decision that has become entangled in the contest between the political imperative to buy European and procurement from elsewhere is the German purchase of NH-90 helicopters.[69] With the announcement in June 2000 that Germany would not purchase the engines for the helicopter from General Electric Aircraft but rather, in a $240m order, from Rolls-Royce, a storm of protest erupted.[70]

Despite UK surprise at these German decisions, London too showed that the trend in Europe is towards buying at home. In May

2000, the Ministry of Defence announced that it would spend £800m on the *Meteor* beyond-visual-range air-to-air missile to arm the 232 *Eurofighter* jets it has ordered.[71] This came as a blow to Raytheon Corporation, which had hoped to win the contract. The Ministry further decided to purchase 25 Airbus A400-Ms for a reported cost of £3.5bn. Until the Airbuses were ready, however, the Ministry would lease C-17s from Boeing for $750m. The decision was nonetheless seen as a major disappointment for the United States, because there had been nearly a year of intense lobbying on the issue.[72] Since the British announcement, the German Defence Ministry has indicated that it might prefer an enhanced version of a Raytheon missile, somewhat countering the momentum towards procurement in Europe.

However, given the sinking defence budget and the lack of clarity over how Germany will finance the procurement intentions described above, the issue is essentially a moot one. Investigating procurement intentions in detail is not yet worthwhile, since the money to turn intentions into orders is simply not there.

Summary: The State of *Bundeswehr* Reform

In summary, the actual content of German military reform will not yield a *Bundeswehr* all that different from the one that currently exists. Scharping has endorsed the goals, present in all proposals for reform, of making the *Bundeswehr* lighter, more mobile and better able to respond quickly to crises. These are all laudable goals. Unfortunately, as reform plans stand at the time of writing, Germany will not reach them, and will continue to make do with the equipment procured under the old paradigm of a heavy territorial defence force with limited mobility.

The problem, as revealed by the early stages of implementation, is partly conceptual (continued prioritisation of classical territorial defence, as opposed to force projection to prevent or curtail crises abroad) and partly financial (on-going lack of funding for reforms). These two issues are irreconcilable. If Germany wants to modernise a large territorial defence force and fulfil its NATO commitments as well, then it needs to increase its military budget. If it wants to shrink its budget, then it needs to abandon its cherished conscription/*Zivi* programmes and downsize radically. At the moment it is trying to maintain a large force while reducing its budget, which simply will not work. The next chapter will explore the consequences of this failure for ESDP.

Chapter 3

The Consequences of German Military Reform for ESDP and NATO

By virtue of its size, economic might and geographical location, Germany will always remain central to any initiative or project that is aimed at addressing European security concerns. While still unfinished, the course and outcome of *Bundeswehr* reform are already raising questions about the prospects for a strengthening of European military capabilities as envisaged in the plans for a fully fledged ESDP. German military reform will of necessity also have an impact on the evolution of NATO and, by extension, transatlantic relations. This chapter considers in greater detail the possible implications of *Bundeswehr* reform for EU military capabilities and its wider consequences for transatlantic relations.

The Status of ESDP

At its summit meeting in Helsinki in December 1999, the EU announced ambitious steps towards organising deployable forces of its own. While discussions about 'pillars' and 'sharing responsibilities' between Europe and the US had recurred throughout the Cold War era, efforts to create a credible European crisis-reaction capability only gathered serious momentum towards the end of the 1990s. The Berlin ministerial in June 1996 discussed the possibility of making Combined Joint Task Forces (CJTFs) available to Europe under the control of the WEU.[1] The joint UK–French declaration on European Defence, issued at the end of their bilateral summit in St Malo in December 1998, plainly stated that the EU must develop a capacity for autonomous security action – and showed French and British willingness to help make that happen. Shortly thereafter, the Kosovo conflict in the spring of 1999 further concentrated minds on the need to strengthen European capabilities and increase options for independent action. NATO's Kosovo campaign forced European policy-makers to recognise that firstly, the United States had been close to refusing to become involved; and that secondly, Europeans would have been hard-pressed to act on their own if the US had remained aloof. Since it had become apparent that the WEU could not produce the desired capacity, EU members decided at the Cologne summit in June 1999 to make the EU proper the locus of security decision-making. This led in turn to the Helsinki announcement the following December.

What, exactly, was achieved at Helsinki? EU member states agreed at the summit to organise a deployable component of 15 brigades, or approximately 50,000–60,000 troops, ready to go within 60 days and sustainable in-theatre for a year. British EU Commissioner Chris Patten supplemented these plans with the unveiling, on 12 April 2000, of a scheme to establish a civilian rapid-reaction team to work alongside the peacekeeping contingent.[2] At the European Council meeting at Santa Maria da Feira in June 2000, members followed up Patten's announcement with the promise to make available up to 5,000 police officers by 2003 for conflict-prevention and crisis-management missions.[3]

New political institutions came into being as well.[4] The leading organisation is a political and security committee (known by the acronym COPS) in Brussels, comprising national representatives of senior/ambassadorial level. This committee is accompanied by a Military Committee (MC), which meets at the level of the Chiefs of Defence Staff as and when necessary. In addition, a permanent EU Military Staff (EUMS) within the Council structure provides military expertise and support, particularly to the conduct of EU-led military crisis-management operations. This staff has as its goal preparation for future Petersberg tasks.[5] However, EUMS is essentially a secretariat, not a command staff. It does not conduct operational planning or have access to secure information.[6]

In early 2001, a British think-tank, the Centre for European Reform, called these actions 'Europe's Military Revolution'.[7] However, these steps, while sensible and laudable, hardly merit the name 'revolution'. Calling for a 'European army' would have been revolutionary. Yet this is precisely what did not happen at Helsinki. Finnish President Martti Ahtisaari went to special pains to emphasise this point at the press conference immediately following the summit, stressing that European goals for the establishment of security capabilities were limited. They should in no way cause suspicion within NATO, he argued, precisely because they did not include the creation of a supranational military organisation.[8]

These steps towards the goal of creating an EU security capacity (often referred to in shorthand as 'the Headline Goal', or HG) are modest ones. Uninformed American emissaries to Europe receive sound rebukes if they use the phrase 'European army' to describe it when speaking with their European counterparts. The HG neither calls for nor establishes a European army, or even a force in the strict military sense of the word, that is, a dedicated unit of troops with a commander. Rather, the HG is, in effect, a menu of options from which EU member-state leaders will one day be able to choose as needed.

During the French EU presidency, progress was made on the HG with the convening of the Capabilities Commitment Conference (CCC) in Brussels on 20–21 November 2000. Fifteen defence ministers met with their allied counterparts from the non-EU member states and with those from candidate states for accession to the EU. The scheduling was clearly driven by a desire not to let a year pass after the December 1999 Helsinki announcement without some kind of demonstrable progress. At the conference, French Defence Minister Alain Richard pointed out it was the first time that a meeting of the so-called '15+15' had been held at the ministerial level.[9] (The term '15+15' refers to the fifteen EU countries plus the six NATO members outside North America that are not in the EU – the Czech Republic, Iceland, Hungary, Norway, Poland and Turkey – plus the nine EU applicants – Bulgaria, Cyprus, Estonia, Latvia, Lithuania, Malta, Slovakia, Slovenia and Romania.[10])

With the exception of Denmark, the participants pledged national troop and equipment commitments to the HG. The conference established a so-called 'force catalogue', including 400 combat aircraft and 100 vessels. Other committed assets include national and multinational headquarters elements.[11] According to the official documentation released afterwards, the conference established a 'satisfactory number of national or multinational headquarters at strategic, operational, force and component levels'.[12] It further established a Headline Task Force (known as HTF) to oversee future developments in cooperation with the EUMS and NATO (referred to as 'HTF+' when NATO experts participate). The guiding principle is the 'preservation of the Union's autonomy in decision-making'.[13]

While impressive on paper, upon closer inspection some of the CCC's shortcomings become more apparent. The number of troops committed (80,000), most of whom are already double-hatted, having been offered to the UN and NATO, will not be sufficient to cover support and rotations for a year of the promised 60,000-strong deployable force. Sustaining such a force in the field for the length of time desired will require three to four times that number of troops, or twice as many as were pledged.[14] While the committed headquarters and combat aircraft seem sufficient, there remain gaps, especially in areas of theatre transport, suppression of enemy air defences (SEAD), and electronic warfare, as well as strategic airlift and sealift.[15] The EU clearly needs to improve its capabilities in these costly areas, including airborne refuelling and strategic intelligence.[16]

Another unresolved issue is how to ensure that EU member states receive better value for money in their defence procurement. François Heisbourg has argued persuasively that the problem is not insufficient defence spending in Europe as a whole, but rather insufficiently wise spending. The problem with the European action in Kosovo was not so much a lack of, say, aircraft, as a lack of other necessary support services that wiser procurement could have provided. Although European member states' defence budgets together amount to approximately 60% of that of the United States, the return is vastly lower.[17] A major reason for this is the continued commitment in Europe to territorially based force structures (of which the *Bundeswehr* is a prominent example), and a willingness to rely on the support of the US.

These problems notwithstanding, the Nice summit of December 2000 went ahead and approved the work of the CCC and a controversial French presidency report on European security. To the dismay of not only the Americans but also the British, the French presidency report once again used the contentious phrase 'an autonomous security capacity'. Partly for this reason, the Nice meeting failed to answer some important questions about the roles of both the EU member states and NATO in creating a capacity that would ideally be separable but not separate.[18] The most controversial issue was the question of what rights of access an EU force would have to NATO assets. The presidency report insisted on wide-ranging guarantees of access. Yet a key NATO member – Turkey – was unwilling to provide such guarantees, despite heavy international pressure.[19] Only grudgingly, after half a year of talks, did Ankara strike a deal at the Budapest meeting of NATO foreign ministers at the end of May 2001. However, the chances are high that its obstructionist policy in this regard will continue, particularly if its prospects for EU membership wane.

Implications of *Bundeswehr* Reform for ESDP

What impact will *Bundeswehr* reform have on ESDP? Specifically, what impact will it have on the ability of the EU to fulfil its goal of creating an effective rapid-reaction force capable of handling 'Petersberg tasks'?

Spokesmen for the German Defence Ministry and Chancellery promise that Germany will contribute its fair share. In public comments, Rudolf Scharping even indicated at one point a German intent ultimately to provide 20% of the rapid-reaction force capability.[20] However, proclamations of the German Defence Ministry aside, will the *Bundeswehr* reform as outlined really allow for that?

As indicated above, there are real doubts about German willingness to foot the bill, given decreasing military spending. Almost as soon as Scharping's mention of 20% became public, a senior German diplomat to the EU told reporters that Scharping's promise was 'meaningless' because there would not be any forces designated for assignment to the EU.[21] Rather, German operational troops could be called upon not only by the EU but also by NATO, and for multinational operations headed by the UN. Such double- and triple-hatting meant that there would be many practical difficulties (which, admittedly, would not be unique to Germany).

General Klaus Naumann, who was chairman of NATO's military committee for most of the Kosovo crisis and was formerly Inspector General of the *Bundeswehr*, casts doubts not only on German contributions, but also on the HG in its entirety. He argued that the EU needs a decade to build up a real military intervention capability, not the three years envisioned in Helsinki.[22] Similarly, Heisbourg argues that what Europe needs is more investment in, and a larger budget for, the tools of force projection. Given that no EU member is currently increasing defence spending in real terms, Heisbourg's wish will probably remain unfulfilled. The decline of the German defence budget is of particular importance. German ability to reshape its forces along the lines of the UK and France will play a 'major role in determining the success or failure of DCI and NATO's ability to adapt to the future', Heisbourg believes. In short, Germany's credibility and image as a good EU and NATO partner is now in question in an unprecedented way.

Some dissenting voices express the view that, even if German reform does not produce significant changes in the near future, it would not matter much for fulfilment of the HG because that goal is so limited, and there are many other nations to pitch in. In this view, if EU member states are willing to continue spending collectively around $170bn or $180bn on defence, they should be able to achieve the HG without straining. The United States, with a budget of roughly $300bn per year, produces forces that can circle the globe; therefore a sum of more than half that should be able to produce a capability with regional scope.[23] A clear case for rationalisation would be to cease spending money via 15 defence budgets and 15 military bureaucracies, but sovereignty issues obviously check any such move.

Another problem specifically involving Germany is the political interaction between ESDP and EU enlargement. NATO is aware that non-EU NATO members' goodwill towards ESDP is necessary, since the EU rapid-reaction force will rely on NATO assets to carry out its missions. Turkish hesitancy about guaranteeing EU access to NATO assets in its area brought the process to a standstill temporarily, and could still be a spanner in the works of an actual operation. The issue of Turkey's attitudes particularly affects Germany because of its large Turkish-immigrant population.

There are also concerns among aspiring EU members that security considerations could pose new requirements for entry into the EU. Once again, this issue particularly concerns Germany, because the aspirant countries are its neighbours and trading partners. For example, a senior Czech official hopes that new security capabilities will not place additional obstacles to the accession of East Central European countries to the EU. Such obstacles could come in the form of expected contributions to a security capacity that the poorer states of the former Warsaw Pact could not fulfil, or potential nervousness among the major European powers about expanding the borders of the areas for which they will be militarily responsible.[24] For its part, Poland wonders about the potential impact on its relations with the United States.[25] Warsaw's pro-American stance has already created friction with France in advance of Poland's even becoming an EU member.

In short, there are a daunting number of open questions about the HG, despite the time elapsed since it was publicised in December 1999. Unfortunately, the uncertain prospects for *Bundeswehr* reform mean that Germany will be unable to assume a leadership role in creating European security capabilities in the short to mid-term. Add to this the uncertainties about the ESDP venture as a whole, as exemplified by the way that the CCC fell short, and the future does not look promising.

Implications of *Bundeswehr* Reform for NATO

What are the implications of *Bundeswehr* reform for Germany's relationship with NATO? The reform clearly does not prepare Germany to fulfil its pre-existing commitments to NATO, which are to achieve readiness for involvement in one Article V conflict at the same time as two non-Article V crises (potentially in south-eastern Europe or the Mediterranean). Nor does it prepare Germany to take on a leadership role in NATO's new tasks. The Washington Strategic Concept added the need to respond to crises and develop partnerships with countries formerly hostile to the principle of common defence.[26]

To encourage all of its allies to meet these commitments, NATO implemented the Defence Capabilities Initiative (DCI). This initiative calls for European nations to fulfil specific goals in five areas: deployability and mobility (DM); sustainability and logistics (SL); NATO consultation, command and control (CC); effective engagement (EE); and survivability of forces and infrastructure (SF). The initiative laid down specific NATO force requirements and target force goals for all NATO countries.

Now the pressure is on Germany to live up to those capabilities, particularly as a role model to other European laggards. As usual, US ambivalence manifests itself in all discussions on the issue. On the one hand, success in creating ESDP would free the US to redirect its energies toward its 'global campaign' against terrorism. On the other hand, there is continuing anxiety, discussed earlier, about the implications of Europe acting with too much independence.

The DCI was updated in June 2000 via a classified document known as MC400/2. This document defined specific capabilities needed by NATO to meet the three primary goals it had established for itself in Washington: collective defence; out-of-area peacekeeping; and peacetime cooperation between NATO and partner countries. The document called for, instead of an eastward line of defence, 'protection against threats from any direction'.[27] It also set down specifics for how NATO should conduct multinational operations out-of-area.

Bundeswehr reform currently will not enable Germany to achieve readiness for the scenarios to which it has agreed. The problem is not the direction of the reform but rather the lack of financing for it, and the lack of a sense of urgency about the issue. Fulfilling DCI goals will require costly procurement commitments. Many of them – such as the need for aerial refuelling capabilities – are, as a German senior official points out, extremely new concerns to a country used to relying on others for such assets.[28] Moreover, the Washington strategic concept calls for maintaining forces in all allied countries at the 'lowest levels consistent with the requirements of collective defence'.[29] In German eyes, this necessitates the maintenance of conscription, a view not shared by major allies.

At least the overall shift in the direction of a smaller *Bundeswehr* with an enlarged operational contingent does conform to the spirit of the strategic concept. Nor are all of the areas in which there is a gap between the US and Germany high-technology ones. Some gaps could be remedied by commercial off-the-shelf (COTS) technology available in Europe, such as materiel for logistics, communication and even lift. Hence it comes down to a question of a willingness to spend the money to acquire those assets.

In addition to the technological and spending gaps, there also appears to be a political gap that will render the process of creating a European consensus for fulfilling the DCI more difficult. Gernot Erler, a member of the *Bundestag* for the SPD and deputy leader of the parliamentary groups, echoes the sentiments of his colleagues in London and Paris when he says that Kosovo, for example, showed dramatically that, when push came to shove, American intelligence was for American eyes only.[30] The common complaint appears to be not that this was entirely unfair or unexpected, given how much more the United States was contributing to the action in Kosovo, but rather that it confirmed the need for Europeans to develop their own intelligence-gathering capabilities. As one senior official at the British Ministry of Defence put it, 'the incentivising effect was large'.[31] Or, as a defence expert for the SPD in Germany similarly expressed it, intelligence sharing among allies is like a bazaar – he who has nothing, receives nothing.[32] Also, the perception that the US has a cavalier attitude towards international law, and indeed sees itself as above it, tends to unsettle not only European political élites but also voters.

It also lies at the heart of French unwillingness to commit in writing to a right of first refusal for NATO on any proposed EU security ventures. A British senior official who often mediates between the French and the Americans on security issues explained that, for the French, 'this implies a servant–master relationship'.[33] The French goal is to avoid preconditions under which the EU can or cannot act. According to the French military attaché in London, it is not even a question of setting a level, above which NATO would be involved and below which the EU would take over. It concerns fundamental questions of European independence.[34]

This was further emphasised for the French when the second Bush administration made clear that it was no longer a question of whether, but of how, to deploy a missile defence. A further source of tension is the manner in which the Bush administration is trying to make missile defence palatable to Europeans. In the wake of the terrorist attacks of September 2001, Washington appears to have lost faith in the concept of deterrence. Even before the attacks, the Bush administration made clear its intent to abandon the ABM Treaty. Yet, deterrence remains a cherished concept in Europe, as does the ABM Treaty. Another problematic US marketing strategy is the notion that missile defence should become 'AMD' – allied missile defence, with shared costs. Given the fact that no European country is increasing defence spending in real terms, none of them wants to be asked for financial contributions to a programme for which there is no domestic constituency.

The US has gained much sympathy in the wake of 11 September. Europeans have a new appreciation of the dangers that the US faces as the only remaining global power and biggest target for terrorists. Yet American diplomats could garner even more goodwill. They could stress that the Bush administration is serious about the possibility of deep cuts in offensive nuclear weapons as part of its nuclear rethink. Cynics, or perhaps simply Russians, could then even declare that this would be a massive silver lining to the missile defence cloud: to placate its allies, the US might make real cuts in its offensive arsenal, gaining in return only the right to conduct decades of uncertain missile defence research leading to the construction of a leaky shield.

Summary

Both conceptually (the prioritisation of territorial defence) and practically (the inadequate reform budget), *Bundeswehr* reform is ill-suited to enabling Germany to pull its weight in ESDP to the same degree as the UK and France. The implications for NATO are similar. Whether or not Germany will achieve the necessary capability to handle agreed NATO commitments remains doubtful. The public admission in spring 2001 that the *Bundeswehr* was no longer fully operational and no longer capable of fulfilling all of its alliance obligations muddied the waters further. Scharping's statement that he would attempt to cut costs by decreasing readiness and backing down from NATO commitments gives little cause for optimism.

One might be tempted to dismiss these claims as an attempt to 'cry wolf' and therefore convince Hans Eichel to loosen the purse strings and increase defence spending. This would be a mistake. These claims are accurate. Moreover, the main cause of *Bundeswehr* deficiencies, insufficient funding, will not change in the foreseeable future. This state of affairs rightly causes annoyance among Germany's NATO and EU allies, who point to agreements already signed by Germany requiring force projection. As shown above, German policy-makers and strategists remain firmly attached to territorial defence as a leading priority. Yet on paper at least Germany has doctrinally committed itself to becoming – as unpleasant as the term may sound – an interventionist power. Whether via the Petersberg tasks (agreed on German soil) or the Helsinki summit, Germany has already signed up doctrinally to a force-projection approach. It has committed to NATO scenarios. Now that NATO has invoked Article V, German allies are justified in criticising Berlin for not taking clearer action to live up to its commitments.

Conclusion

German Military Reform and European Security

The process of German military reform has not run its course and the future role of the *Bundeswehr*, both in relation to German society and to European security and defence policy, continues to be a subject of debate within Germany. Still, as this paper has shown, the general direction that military reform is taking and the complex of factors influencing the reform process are clear enough. What are the implications for Germany's NATO allies and for European efforts to fashion a more autonomous defence capability?

Policy Implications for Germany's Allies

A worthwhile first step would be for Washington to stop worrying about any potentially decoupling effects of the European Headline Goal. The HG does not create a European army; it does not even create a force in the strict military sense of the word, that is, a unique group of soldiers and commanders. Rather, it creates a menu of options from which European leaders will be able to choose in order to manage a particular crisis at any given point. Put bluntly, the HG creates a list of phone numbers, not an army.

Moreover, that list will remain limited without sizeable German contributions. However, Berlin has yet to show that it will make such contributions. As a result, rather than worrying about Europe doing too much on its own, Americans should continue to be concerned about Europe, and particularly Germany, doing too little.

Next, it is worth bearing in mind the influence of history upon the German attitude towards military modernisation. The notion that history decrees a professional military to be too dangerous for Germany to handle remains pervasive. Similarly, when Germany's NATO allies express disappointment about the *Bundeswehr*'s small combat role in Kosovo, or lacking ability to project force, they must remember the historical roots of Germany's dislike for interventionist military campaigns.

In essence, the 'starting point' for the *Bundeswehr* on its path to becoming a more mobile intervention force is a very different one to that of its French or British counterparts. Such a transition goes against the founding charter not only of the *Bundeswehr*, but also of the *Bundesrepublik*, the Federal Republic of Germany, as a whole. This charter was imposed originally by the victorious powers after the Second World War, but became, and remains, widely accepted. German political leaders from all parties, from Volker Rühe to Joschka Fischer, have succeeded in overcoming this historical charter to a certain extent, by creating a political willingness for out-of-area German combat involvement. The courts have certified that these actions have been constitutional. As a result, when push came to shove, despite numerous difficulties, Germans got to Kosovo and completed the jobs given to them. These were notable achievements; they deserve more recognition abroad than they have received.

However, the German involvement in Kosovo marked both a success and a failure for the German Federal Ministry of Defence. It was a success in that Germany was there at all, but a failure in that it clearly demonstrated the major shortcomings in the *Bundeswehr*'s ability to deploy appropriate forces rapidly. The course of military reform so far has not convincingly shown that the *Bundeswehr* will correct these shortcomings.

The problem is not a lack of willingness to reform. The Defence Ministry has made clear its intention to increase the size of its operational component and to provide it with both more modern and more appropriate support and lift. However, two crucial problems remain:

- The first is the source of the financing, which remains unclear. In an era of budget- and tax-cutting in Berlin, and in light of Scharping's public announcements that he would maintain both conscription and the majority of Germany's hundreds of small bases, the only major avenue left for financing is through the *Bundeswehr*'s own attempts to save money, sell assets and function more efficiently. Rumours in summer 2001 that the *Bundeswehr* was considering using its property to secure loans from the open market suggested that few other solutions are available. Whether these ideas will pay for the reforms is unclear at best.

- Second, it is not sufficient to view budgetary issues as the sole reason why German military reform will not fulfil its goals. The United States, the UK and France need to understand that Germany is committed to European security, but has a different view of what that commitment requires. Germany never stopped prioritising homeland defence, and remains worried about instability in Russia. It views its financial contributions to economic stability in the former East Germany and former Warsaw Pact as part of its contribution to improving European security, one which it wants its allies to take into account when they criticise the decreasing defence budget allocations.

It must be emphasised that these are not *a priori* the 'wrong priorities'. For example, maintaining conscription does not, in the abstract, condemn the *Bundeswehr* to immobility. Conscripts are not inherently unusable, although in practice they have been shown to be undeployable in many circumstances. Likewise, strict budget management with an eye to reducing the amount of German debt, especially when the government .has to take on DM10bn in new debt every year to service its aging population, makes sense. But it does not allow for the necessary increases in defence spending.

Perhaps the best way to summarise these German choices is to say that they prioritise domestic concerns above international ones. Moreover, when pressed to show their commitment to NATO, German defence experts often reply by citing numbers, such as the fact that Germany has the largest standing army in Europe, or that large numbers of German troops are currently deployed in the Balkans. In contrast, discussions in London, Paris and Washington tend to centre on capability rather than size.

Yet for German policy-makers, conscription remains a necessary component of both domestic and allied security. Just as the

British and Americans question the preparedness of conscripts, Germans question the motives and merits of professional soldiers. Such questioning causes unnecessary tensions on both sides. Germany's allies wonder about the deployability of German conscripts and the implied denigration of professional forces. German leaders feel resentment at the pressure from abroad to increase spending and follow its allies' examples in reform.

In summary, there is no lack of awareness in Germany of the need to reform its military forces and contribute to the improvement of European security capabilities. However, that awareness takes Germany in different directions from those that its allies might presume for it, and remains hostage to an inter-governmental and more specifically inter-party struggle (an increasingly personal one between Eichel and Scharping) about the budget. While terrorism has produced renewed interest in homeland defence in the US, such defence is defined as the ability to counter foes around the globe. Germany does not have the same definition. The consequences are that Germany will not develop the capabilities that its allies might hope for.

Increasing the Pressure or Lowering Expectations?

If they are unwilling simply to accept the status quo, what can Germany's allies do about it? One school of thought would suggest that now, in the wake of 11 September 2001, the US could lean heavily on Berlin and insist that it contribute more to NATO. Sometimes straight talking can work. However, given the accumulated resentment that has already developed on the issue of improving German military capabilities, the danger is high that such talk would be counter-productive.

Berlin has a point in that Britain, France and the United States sometimes forget the budgetary constraints brought about by unification, which, far from being complete, remains an enormous and costly on-going project. On top of this, Germany's key allies must bear in mind that the view from the front line of the Cold War was different. This experience on the front line lingers in German minds even though it is gone from the maps. As the country's diplomats abroad emphasise, continuity is a central concept in German foreign policy – and that extends to strategic assessment.

Hence a more realistic policy would be to lower expectations regarding both when and to what extent Germany will be able to increase its contributions to NATO's new missions and to ESDP. Both NATO and the EU may be pleasantly surprised by the ability of the *Bundeswehr* to save money by functioning more like a private business. At the same time, Washington should redouble its efforts to improve the state of US–French relations. The intervention in Kosovo proved France's ability to perform as a capable, competent and reliable security partner. The same was true of the British, but the UK does not enjoy the same political weight on the continent as France, which matters when the issue at hand is the evolution of an EU security force. Upgrading France's status in security matters may actually improve US–French relations. There is a sense in Washington that the US missed a precious opportunity in the mid-1990s by not welcoming France more warmly back to NATO and not treating it more seriously as a security partner at that time. The US should aim to redress that failing.

The policy prescription is more difficult within the EU. There, the best approach would be not so much to lower policy expectations as to lower public expectations. The unique EU culture of evolving consensus through consultation is a proven model, but it does take time. The EU should extend its timeline for the creation of a rapid-reaction capability beyond the current unrealistic date of 2003 and continue to work with Germany and other member states out of the public view to generate willingness for increased defence spending. Such an effort will require more time than is currently being allowed. In the meantime, the US will continue to carry out tasks that ESDP might one day perform.

These issues have resonance far beyond the small community of élite foreign-policy makers. The events in former Yugoslavia since the end of the Cold War have shown clearly what capabilities the leading European military powers, and eventually the EU itself, need. For all of the rhetoric about creating new capacities, the post-Helsinki ESDP is instead shaping up to be a more organised means of filling old gaps. In other words, it will allow European nations to rotate in and out of the Balkans in a more systematic fashion than in the 1990s – desirable, but hardly ground-breaking. Ideally, ESDP would go beyond such rotations and produce the capacity to handle the full spectrum of Petersberg tasks and more. This is in fact the stated declaration of the EU. As the Swedish presidency report issued from the Göteborg summit in June 2001 put it, 'The Helsinki Headline Goal for the development of military capabilities aims to enable the EU by 2003 to deploy rapidly and then sustain forces capable of the full range of Petersberg tasks, including the most demanding.'[1] In a best-case scenario, it would serve as a 'Petersberg-plus' capability, one that could also contribute substantially to the campaign against terrorism.

Yet the reality so far looks very different. Without a significant German contribution, ESDP will remain at the level of 'Petersberg-minus'. The success of ESDP will rest primarily on the ability of the UK, France and Germany to pull their respective weights. The test of the fire-fight in Kosovo has shown convincing UK and French potential to do so. It did not show the same for Germany. Although Berlin is aware of the need to redress this problem, the lack of funding and emphasis on territorial defence mean that it will not do so in the near future. Until German defence planners face the difficult reality that they must either increase spending, or give up long-cherished institutions such as conscription and widely scattered small base placements, ESDP will remain simply a better organised means of maintaining the status quo.

Appendix

Excerpts from Key Reform Guidelines

The 'Weizsacker Commission' Report

Excerpt from the report by the Commission on the Common Security and Future of the *Bundeswehr* [Weizsäcker Commission] to the federal government: 'A Fundamental Renewal' (*Gemeinsame Sicherheit und Zukunft der Bundeswehr, Bericht der Kommission an die Bundesregierung*), (23 May 2000).

1. For the first time in its history, Germany is surrounded on all sides solely by allies and integration partners and faces no threat to its territory from neighbours. This new basis of German security is not of a transitory nature, but will remain valid for the foreseeable future.

...

2. Proceeding from this basis, the independent Commission on the 'Common Security and the Future of the *Bundeswehr*' appointed by the federal government embarked upon the task of examining the risks and interests of the Federal Republic of Germany in the field of security and of issuing recommendations on how Germany's armed forces can in the future perform their duties within the framework of an inclusive security and defence policy. The principal task was to draw up proposals for the basic structures of a new *Bundeswehr*.

...

3. Four demands had to be reconciled during the commission's studies, namely, to find the best medium and long-term solution to the problem of how to construct a (1) functional *Bundeswehr* fit for employment in an alliance role on the basis of a (2) socially acceptable form of military service and to provide it [*sic*] (3) technologically up-to-date equipment within (4) appropriate budgetary bounds.

...

4. The *Bundeswehr* as it is in the year 2000 is off-balance with regard to these demands. It is too big, ill-composed and increasingly out of step with the times. The *Bundeswehr* has no future in its current structure. The present form of military service produces a surplus of manpower altogether, but a shortage of operational forces. Out-dated material diminishes its operational capability and causes operating costs to soar. The current budget estimates allow no scope for adequate modernisation under the present structure and form of military service. The contributions to the internationally agreed tasks assured by Germany's policy-makers cannot be provided by its armed forces, at least not in the longer run. Even today, the operational forces are overtaxed in terms of both manpower and material.

...

7. From the lessons learned in operations in recent years and the comparison made with our major partners, the commission comes to the conclusion that the yardstick for the new *Bundeswehr* should be the capability to participate in up to two crisis response operations simultaneously and indefinitely – with operational forces on the following scale:

The Army: Two brigade-size operational contingents with the requisite support and command elements (a total of up to 16,000 troops).

The Air Force: Two operational contingents with a total of 90 to 100 combat aircraft, 10 ground-based air defence squadrons, as well as aerial refuelling and airlift components.

The Navy: Two operational contingents composed of ships, submarines and aircraft and capable of conducting combined naval warfare operations.

The Medical Service: Two operational contingents with mobile hospital and medical evacuation capacities.

To perform these tasks, including assuring a due exchange of the troops deployed, the operational forces in the *Bundeswehr* must be reinforced from the present figure of around 60,000 to some 140,0000. These forces – with the support of a basic military organisation numbering around 100,000 personnel – will also enable Germany to pull its weight in Alliance defence.

...

9. ...The peacetime strength of the *Bundeswehr* should be oriented to a standard figure of 240,000 troops. The commission recommends that a 10-month term of basic military service be retained and that the number of conscripts called up to do their basic military service in the future be oriented on the reduction in the number required by the armed forces. What this amounts to in effect is a form of military service based on selection. Those performing this service should receive higher compensation.

...

10. To enable the federal government to make progress towards the security and defence policy objectives stated, the commission recommends this catalogue of measures:

i. The structure of the armed forces should be oriented on the tasks they will most likely have to perform within the context of **crisis prevention and crisis management** – to be able to fulfil national and Alliance defence requirements and meet international commitments.

ii. The armed forces should be reorganised to produce an **operational force component** of 140,000 troops that is **functional and fit for employment in an alliance role**.

iii. The **peacetime strength** of the armed forces should be **reduced** to a standard figure of 240,000 troops, including an annual figure of 30,000 conscripts on a 10-month term of military service.

iv. The **build-up potential** should be used to achieve a **wartime strength** of 300,000 troops and a manpower reserve of 100,000 troops.

v. The number of **civilian personnel posts** should be **reduced** to around 80,000, with an appropriate reduction in tasks, services and garrisons or bases.

vi. The **command structures** should be reorganised and streamlined to allow effective command and control; the responsibility of the **Chief of Staff of the** *Bundeswehr* for *Bundeswehr* planning, command and control and acquisition should be enhanced; all the **ministerial functions** should be centralised and discharged **in Berlin**.

vii. **Controlling** should be introduced as an instrument at the disposal of the Executive Group at the ministry.

viii. All joint, territorial and supporting functions should be grouped together and discharged by **a new organisation known as the Central Military Services**.

...

The 'Scharping' Report

Excerpt from the report by the German Minister of Defence: 'The *Bundeswehr* – Advancing Steadily into the 21st Century. Cornerstones of a Fundamental Renewal' (*Der Bundesminister der Verteidigung, 'Die Bundeswehr sicher ins 21. Jahrhundert: Eckpfeiler für eine Erneuerung von Grund auf'*), ([end of] May 2000).

The Constitutive Foundations

1. The Basic Law puts Germany under the obligation to serve world peace as an equal part of a united Europe.

2. Article 24 of the Basic Law stipulates that Germany may become a party to a system of collective security and, in doing so, may consent to such limitations upon its sovereign powers as will bring about and secure a peaceful and lasting order in Europe and among the nations of the world.

As a member of the North Atlantic Alliance, the Western European Union and the European Union, Germany makes a contribution to security insurance in the Euro-Atlantic area that is based on an assured defence capability and commensurate with its political and economic weight. This includes the obligation to take part in conflict prevention and crisis-management measures carried out under the auspices of the Alliance and the United Nations as well as commitment to protecting international human rights.

3. The fundamental mission of German armed forces is, as stated in Article 87a of the Basic Law, national defence. Germany, however, has gone beyond that and, under Article 5 of the North Atlantic Treaty and Article V of the Brussels Treaty, accepted a binding commitment to render assistance within the framework of collective defence.

…

The Mission of the *Bundeswehr*

The *Bundeswehr*

- protects Germany and its citizens against political blackmail and danger from without,
- defends Germany and its allies,
- contributes to the preservation of peace and stability in the Euro-Atlantic area,
- advances world peace and international security in accordance with the Charter of the United Nations,
- provides disaster relief, saves life and supports humanitarian activities.

…

Equipment and Material

47. The equipment held by the *Bundeswehr* will be fully modernised. The capability profile derived from the changed security environment, the international commitments, the mission laid down in the constitution, the Defence Capabilities Initiative and the European Headline Goal set the priorities for the issue of material and for acquisition.

Planning leeway will be created by the rigorous performance of tasks on a joint basis.

48. Top priority will be assigned to improving strategic deployability. Our aim is to build up and manage air and sea transport capacities in cooperation with our European partners.

The *Bundeswehr* will acquire a space-borne reconnaissance capability of its own to improve Germany's capacity to assess political and military situations and to supplement Alliance capabilities.

Second priority will go to fielding high-performance, compatible communication and command and control facilities, these being pacemakers for interoperability and a basic requirement for establishing a joint and combined system network.
...

Universal Conscription

59. National defence is the core mission of German armed forces. It can also only be ensured in the future through universal conscription. Universal conscription is an element of Germany's security insurance and will continue to be indispensable.

60. The draft is a major disruption in the lives of German young men. They must not be taxed by military service any longer than is necessary to guarantee the external security of our country and the readiness of the armed forces. Military service must also take whatever account possible of the professional and private plans of the conscripts.

61. Developments in security provide leeway for flexibility in the performance of military service. The changed overall situation and attendant extensions in political warning times and periods available for military preparations will be taken into consideration in the intensity of the training and the readiness of the forces for national defence in an Alliance context.
The legal duration of basic military service will fundamentally be 9 months in the future. The young men drafted will have the possibility of performing their basic military service in one go on posts that are required for keeping the armed forces running in peacetime. They will be assigned posts close to their homes and associated with their professions and will not be under any obligation to do further active-duty training.

62. Alongside this, there will be the option of performing basic military service in stages. Young men who decide in favour of this will perform a six-month period of military service in which they will be conveyed basic military knowledge and skills they will need for national defence purposes. They will be obliged to

undergo active-duty training over the following years to broaden these basic qualifications.

...

Overview of Implementation Plans

Excerpt from the report by the German Minister of Defence, 'New Organization for the Bundeswehr: Overview of Plans, Findings, and Decisions' (*Der Bundesminister der Verteidigung, 'Neuausrichtung der Bundeswehr: Grobausplanung, Ergebnisse und Entscheidungen', Verteidigungsministerium*), (October 2000).

As of the time of writing, this document was available only in German. Translations below are the author's own.

Preface

With the approval of the fundamentals of reform on 14 June 2000, and of the budget for the year 2001 on 21 June 2000, the cabinet of the federal government [of Germany] approved the framework and basis for a thorough reform of the *Bundeswehr*.

With a directive on 29 June 2000, the Federal Defence Minister initiated the planning for the reform of both fighting forces and administration.

As a first step in this process, the overview below was prepared at the end of September [2000].

Its most important findings, and the conclusions that it draws from them, provide the basis for the detailed planning to follow [in later 2000 and 2001], and are described in summary fashion in the pages that follow:

...

Schedule

14–21 June 2000	Cabinet decisions.
29 June 2000	Directive of the Federal Minister [of Defence] to begin the new planning for the *Bundeswehr*.
July–Sept 2000	Overview planning of personnel, structures, tasks, and procedures.

Oct–Dec 2000	Detailed planning of personnel needs and structures.
End 2000	Conceptualisation of equipment needs and procurement.
First half 2001	Devise and seek approval of plans for stationing.
Second half 2001	Begin process of transformation; receive approval of stationing proposals.
End 2001 at latest	Finalise legal and compensation guidelines.

...

Personnel Set-up for Deployment Tasks

- Deployable forces will be increased nearly threefold. In the future, the *Bundeswehr* will have a deployable force of approximately 150,000 soldiers. These troops will fulfil all EU and NATO requirements to which we have agreed. The previous distinction between crisis-reaction forces and main defence forces will be removed.

- The deployable forces will be supported by a basic military organisation [that is, main defence force] of approximately 108,000 soldiers. Their most important tasks will be as follows: national command capability; logistics and support; centralised military training; providing for a continued capacity for territorial defence.

- In addition, approximately 22,000 service positions [*Dienstposten*] for training and in particular for allowing soldiers to receive training in skills useful for civilian employment will be created. ...

- In the future, the total strength of the fighting force will be 280,000 soldiers.

...

Division of Personnel among Services

The services will become smaller and will transfer tasks and personnel to the Medical Service and the new *Streitkräfebasis* [Fighting Force Basis].

For example, 31,000 soldiers will be transferred from the army to the *Streitkräftebasis* and 11,000 will be transferred to the Medical Service.

The numbers mentioned are guidelines. They arise from conceptual guidelines; further determination based on the deployment tasks at hand and a strict leadership organisation will be essential.

The *Bundeswehr* of the future will be able, without resorting to mobilisation and call-ups, to carry out a large operation involving all services over a time period of up to one year, or to carry out two medium-sized operations over a longer time period and in parallel to many small operations.

Notes

Acknowledgements

Numerous individuals and organisations have been of great help in the preparation of this paper. The Ford Foundation provided the funding, for which I am grateful. Sixty policy-makers, strategists and experts in five countries gave generously of their time and insight in allowing me to interview them. Dr Ronald Asmus, Colonel Kathleen Conley, Dr Peter Dombrowski, Brigadier Brian Isbell and Dr Christian Raskob provided much-needed research assistance, as did many in-house colleagues. Phillip Mitchell and Mark Stoker provided expert advice on the tables and Jennifer Knight copy-edited the first draft. Susan Bevan, Sophie Delfolie, Helga Haack, Emma Sullivan and Sheelagh Urbanoviez provided friendly production support throughout. Peter Jukes showed good humour by putting up with me. Finally, this paper is dedicated to the memory of Dr Gerald Segal. One of his last acts was to decide to hire me, and I will always regret that I did not thereafter have the honour of working with him at IISS.

Introduction

[1] Ronald D. Asmus, *Germany's Geopolitical Maturation: Public Opinion and Security Policy in 1994* (Santa Monica CA: RAND, 1995 p. 41).

[2] *Ibid.*, p. 3.

[3] *Bestandsaufnahme Die Bundeswehr an der Schwelle zum 21. Jahrhundert* (Bonn: Bundesministerium der Verteidigung, 1999), pp. 28–30.

[4] Klaus Becher, 'Reforming German Defence', *Survival*, vol. 42, No. 3, Autumn 2000, p. 164.

[5] 'Scharping: Ende des Kosovo-Einsatzes nicht absehbar', *Frankfurter Allgemeine Zeitung*, 23 March 2000. Franz Borkenhagen, Deputy Chief of the Planning Staff in the German Defence Ministry and key adviser to *Bundeswehr* General Inspector Harald Kujat, summarises the change in attitude as follows. Previously Germans could not take part in out-of-area deployments; now, 'it would no longer be justifiable to the international community if German fighting forces did

not take part'. Franz H.U. Borkenhagen, *Außenpolitische Interessen Deutschlands: Rolle und Aufgaben der Bundeswehr* (Bonn: Bouvier Verlag, 1997), p. 197.

6 For more on this issue, see Peter Dombrowski, '*Bundeswehr* Reforms and Transatlantic Security', *Strategic Review*, Fall 2000, pp. 59–65.

7 Gilles Andréani, Christoph Bertram, and Charles Grant, *Europe's Military Revolution* (London: Centre for European Reform, and Paris: Institute for Security Studies, Western European Union, February 2001), p. 2.

Chapter 1

1 David S. Yost, 'The NATO Capabilities Gap and the European Union', *Survival*, vol. 42, Winter 2000–01, p. 120.

2 Kommission Gemeinsame Sicherheit und Zukunft der Bundeswehr, ed., *Summary, Common Security and the Future of the Bundeswehr, Report of the Commission to the Federal Government*' (Multilingual summary of German original) (Bonn: May 2000), p. 12. Available on the *Bundeswehr* website, www.bundeswehr.de

3 'Deutsche Wunschliste für Washington', *Frankfurter Allgemeine Zeitung*, 29 January 2001.

4 'US and NATO Split Over Missile Defense', *International Herald Tribune*, 30 May 2001.

5 On this topic, see also Hanns W. Maull, 'Germany and the Use of Force: Still a "Civilian Power?" ', *Survival*, vol. 42, Summer 2000, pp. 57–8.

6 Interview with the author, Berlin, 10 October 2000.

7 'Deutsch-französische Treffen künftig alle sechs Wochen', *Frankfurter Allgemeine Zeitung*, 2 February 2001.

8 Interview with the author, Bundeskanzleramt, Berlin, 25 May 2000.

9 Constanze Stelzenmüller, 'Rudolf retten bis zur Wahl', *Die Zeit*, 31 May 2001.

10 Interview with the author, Ministry of Defence, London, 22 June 2000.

11 'Scharping warnt vor Abschaffung der Wehrpflicht', *Frankfurter Allgemeine Zeitung*, 15 November 2000.

12 Interview with the author, Auswärtiges Amt, Berlin, 23 May 2000.

13 Interview with the author, Bundeskanzleramt, Berlin, 25 May 2000.

14 Remarks by Richard von Weizsäcker at the presentation of the Weizsäcker Commission Report, Berlin Press Conference Centre, 23 May 2000 (author in attendance).

15 ' "Wir sind nur bedingt einsatzfähig" ', *Der Spiegel*, 29 May 2000, p. 32.

16 Comments of a spokesman for the *Bundeswehrverband*, quoted in 'Bundeswehrverband fordert Bekenntnis zur Wehrpflicht', *Frankfurter Allgemeine Zeitung*, 17 May 2000.

17 'Filter gegen rechts', *Der Spiegel*, 24 February 2001, p. 18.

18 Hans-Dieter Lemke, 'Bundeswehrreform Probleme der Finanzierung', *SWP-aktuell*, vol. 65, October 2000, p. 4.

19 Bundesministerium für Familie, Frauen und Jugend, *Informationen 1999*, no. 140, 20 December 1999.

20 Françoise Manfrass-Sirjacques, *'Die französische Sicherheitspolitik zwischen Anspruch und Wirklichkeit'*, (Hessische Stiftung Friedens- und Konfliktforschung, February 1999), p. 28.

21 'French Defense, NATO and Europe', Speech by Alain Richard, CSIS, Washington DC, 22 February 2000. This issue is also one of the key points in Heisbourg's critique of German military reform proposals, which he terms 'Germany's non-revolution in military affairs'. He argues that the continued presence of conscripts in the *Bundeswehr* 'acts as an element of inertia against participation in high-risk combat operations by ground forces'. See François Heisbourg, 'Germany's Non-Revolution in Military Affairs', *Internationale Politik*, vol. 2, 2000, p. 81.

22 Harald Müller, 'Nuclear Weapons and German Interests: An Attempt at Redefinition', *PRIF Reports*, no. 55 (Peace Research Institute/Hessische Stiftung Friedens- und Konfliktsforschung, August 2000), p. 12.

23 Joschka Fischer faced the delicate challenge of dealing with both Putin and the new US administration in rapid succession in February 2001; see the coverage in 'Der Beginn einer wunderbaren Freundschaft', *Frankfurter Allgemeine Zeitung*, 22 February 2001.

24 'Scharping stößt in Moskau auf Kritik', *Frankfurter Allgemeine Zeitung*, 31 January 2001.

Chapter 2

1 For a biting commentary on the leaked memo affair of May 2001, see Jochen Buchsteiner, 'Schröder's kleiner Kissinger, *Die Zeit*, 23 May 2001.

2 Volker Krönig, MdB, 'Die neue Bundeswehr und der Preis ihrer Reform', *Denkwürdigkeiten, Journal der Politisch-Militärischen Gesellschaft*, vol. 8, September 2000, p. 1.

3 Becher, 'Reforming German Defence', p. 165.

4 Interview with the author, Ministry of Defence, 22 June 2000.

5 Constanze Stelzenmüller, 'Scharpings Affront', *Die Zeit*, 23 March 2000.

6 Kommission Gemeinsame Sicherheit und Zukunft der Bundeswehr, ed., *Summary, Common Security and the Future of the Bundeswehr, Report of the Commission to the Federal Government*, p. 12.

7 *Ibid.*, p. 13.

8 *Ibid.*, p. 14.

9 Remarks at press conference, 23 May 2000.

10 Gemeinsame Sicherheit und Zukunft der Bundeswehr, *Bericht der Kommission an die Bundesregierung*, (full-length German language original report), 23 May 2000, p. 28.

11 Becher, 'Reforming German Defence', p.165.

12 *Bericht der Kommission an die Bundesregierung*, p. 59.

13 *Ibid.*, p. 67.

14 *Ibid.*, p. 69.

15 *Ibid.*, p. 47.

16 *Ibid.*, p. 23.

17 Generalinspekteur der Bundeswehr, *Eckwerte für die konzeptionelle und planerische Weiterentwicklung der*

Streitkräfte, Bundesministerium der Verteidigung, 23 May 2000, p. 6. Available at: www.Bundeswehr.de/ministerium/politik_aktuell/eckwerte.pdf

18 Cited in Becher, 'Reforming German Defence', p. 166.

19 *Eckwerte für die konzeptionelle und planerische Weiterentwicklung der Streitkräfte*, p. 6.

20 *Ibid.*, p. 6.

21 Kujat is regarded by many as too long desk-bound to be personally familiar to the troops in the way Kirchbach was. There is nonetheless a recognition that the political talents of the new general inspector, who took over on 1 July 2000, stand him in good stead.

22 Der Bundesminister der Verteidigung, *Die Bundeswehr sicher ins 21. Jahrhundert: Eckpfeiler für eine Erneuerung von Grund auf*, Verteidigungsministerium, distributed as pamphlet and posted on website, May 2000, p. 3. Also available in English, 'The *Bundeswehr* – Advancing Steadily into the 21st Century. Cornerstones of a Fundamental Renewal' on www.Bundeswehr.de/news/images/cornerstones.doc

23 *Ibid.*, p. 9.

24 'Scharping: Bundeswehr nicht voll bündnisfähig', *Frankfurter Allgemeine Zeitung*, 28 March 2000.

25 Rudolf Scharping, 'Fähig zum Handeln: Wie Europa in der Sicherheitspolitik zum gleichberechtigten Partner Amerikas werden kann', *Die Zeit*, 30 March 2000.

26 'Europäische Sicherheit schwächt die Nato nicht', *Frankfurter Allgemeine Zeitung*, 3 April 2000.

27 *Die Bundeswehr sicher ins 21. Jahrhundert: Eckpfeiler für eine Erneuerung von Grund auf*, p. 26.

28 *Ibid.*, p. 29.

29 'Bundeshaushalt 2001 beschlossen', 22 June 2000, www.bundesregierung.de/homepages/home.html

30 'Eine halbe Milliarde Mark mehr fuer den Verteidigungsminister von 2003 an', *Frankfurter Allgemeine Zeitung*, 31 May 2001.

31 For a useful overview of this problem, see James P. Thomas, *The Military Challenges of Transatlantic Coalitions*, Adelphi Paper no. 333 (Oxford: Oxford University Press for the IISS, May 2000).

32 In July 2000 the British Ministry of Defence announced an increase in military spending from £23bn in 2000 to almost £25bn by 2003–04.

33 A realaudio version of the speech and a summary of the discussion are available on the American Institute for Contemporary German Studies' website, www.aicgs.org. Press spokesman comments made in Berlin on 9 October 2000.

34 Hans-Jürgen Leersch, 'Scharping: Privatisierungen bringen drei zusaetzliche Milliarden', *Die Welt*, 15 June 2001.

35 'Vielen Generälen ist Scharping unheimlich', *Frankfurter Allgemeine Zeitung*, 15 June 2000, p. 2.

36 Admiral Dieter Wellershoff, 'Richtige Lagebeurteilung – unzureichende Konsequenz', *Frankfurter Allgemeine Zeitung*, 5 July 2000. Hanns Maull has also concluded that reform of German capabilities is 'more political than military, more symbolic than real'. 'The

Bundeswehr reforms are unlikely to receive the kind of financial resources and political commitment that they would need, and German security policies will probably continue to be troubled by unresolved strategic issues'. See Hanns W. Maull, 'Germany and the Use of Force: Still a "Civilian Power?" ', p. 57.

37 Michael J. Inacker, 'Militärs: *Bundeswehr* ist nicht bündnisfähig', *Die Welt*, 5 March 2001.

38 IISS, *Strategic Survey 2000–2001* (Oxford: Oxford University Press for the IISS, 2001), p. 106.

39 The entire analysis is worth reading: Hans-Dieter Lemke, 'Bundeswehrreform Probleme der Finanzierung', *SWP-aktuell*, no. 65, October 2000.

40 'Eine halbe Milliarde Mark mehr fuer den Verteidigungsminister von 2003 an', *Frankfurter Allgemeine Zeitung*, 31 May 2001.

41 Constanze Stelzenmüller, 'Rudolf retten – bis zur Wahl'.

42 Karl Feldmeyer, 'Scharpings Prinzip Hoffnung', *Frankfurter Allgemeine Zeitung*, 12 October 2000.

43 François Léotard and Volker Rühe, 'Für eine glaubwürdige Sicherheitspolitik in Europa', *Frankfurter Allgemeine Zeitung*, 31 January 2001. Scharping's own party colleague, parliamentary SPD head Peter Struck, called for Scharping to end the assault on the government's credibility by making clear how he would finance these and future plans. 'Struck dringt auf rasche Klärung der Pläne für Bundeswehr', *Frankfurter Allgemeine Zeitung*, 7 March 2001.

44 Hans-Jürgen Leersch, 'Nur noch begrenzt bündnisfähig', *Die Welt*, 14 June 2001.

45 See, for example, 'Ein Soldat verzweifelt an der Bundeswehr', *Die Welt*, 11 March 2001.

46 Both are available in German on the *Bundeswehr* website, www.Bundeswehr.de. The former is titled 'Grobausplanung' and the latter 'Zwischenbilanz 24.10.00'.

47 'Zwischenbilanz 24.10.00', p. 22.

48 The author is indebted to Brigadier B.R. Isbell, British Embassy, Berlin, for supplying both detailed information on this particular issue and also comments on an earlier draft of this paper.

49 'Grobausplanung', Abschnitt 'Personelle Ausrichtung auf Einsatzaufgaben'.

50 'Grobausplanung', Abschnitt 'Personalaufteilung auf Organisationsbereiche'.

51 'Entscheidung über Bundeswehrstandorte', *Frankfurter Allgemeine Zeitung*, 29 January 2001.

52 'Der Bundestag beschließt zwei Änderungen des Grundgesetzes', *Frankfurter Allgemeine Zeitung*, 28 Oktober 2000.

53 'Grobausplanung', Abschnitt 'Frauen in den Streitkräften/ Bewerbungen'.

54 'Zwischenbilanz 24.10.00', p. 26ff.

55 'Die Bundeswehr will Anteile ausgeben', *Frankfurter Allgemeine Zeitung*, 23 November 2000.

56 For a more detailed analysis of this issue than can be provided here, see Burkard Schmitt, *From Cooperation to Integration: Defence and Aerospace Industries in Europe*, Chaillot Paper 40, Institute for Security Studies, Western European Union, Paris, July 2000.

57 IISS, *The Military Balance 2000–2001* (Oxford: Oxford University Press for the IISS, 2000), p. 42.

58 Hanns W. Maull, 'Germany and the Use of Force: Still a "Civilian Power?" ', p. 73.

59 'Arms Cooperation/European Consolidation', *Atlantic News*, 7 June 2000.

60 John Deutch, Arnold Kanter and Brent Scowcroft, 'Saving NATO's Foundation', *Foreign Affairs*, November/December 1999, pp. 54–5.

61 On US initiatives, then-Secretary of State Madeleine Albright announced, in May 2000, that the US government would streamline its export licensing procedures, and presided over the launch of the US Defense Trade Security Initiative (DTSI) to remove many of the legal and administrative obstacles for a select group of allies. See 'US to Open Up Defence Trade', *FT.com*, 24 May 2000.

62 Interview with the author, Auswärtiges Amt, Berlin, 25 May 2000.

63 Constanze Stelzenmüller, 'Rudolf retten bis zur Wahl'.

64 *The Military Balance 2000–2001*, pp. 38–39.

65 Ulrich Weisser, *Sicherheit für ganz Europe* (Stuttgart: DVA, 1999) p. 243.

66 François Heisbourg, interview with the author, IISS, London, 23 March 2000.

67 'France/Germany: Declaration on Arms Security Cooperation', *Atlantic News*, 15 June 2000.

68 'Berlin und Paris demonstrieren Einigkeit', *Frankfurter Allgemeine Zeitung*, 10 June 2000.

69 When Domenico Cipicchio, the Pentagon's deputy director of defense procurement, travelled to Germany in the week of 8 May 2000, he was distressed by the 'implementation of source selection criteria' and the German introduction of a 'preferred customer requirement'. The US Ambassador in Germany at the time, John Kornblum, wrote personally to the Deputy Defense Minister, Walter Stützle, to protest about the fact that 'political–industrial pressure is attempting to slant the playing field toward' a European purchasing option. 'US Charges European Bias in Engine Buy', *Defense News*, 22 May 2000.

70 'Losers Complain Politics Steered Germany's Engine Choice for NH-90', *Defense News*, 19 June 2000.

71 'UK Defense Deal is Boost to Europeans', *Wall Street Journal*, 17 May 2000.

72 'Britain's US-Missile Rebuff May Cause Uproar', *Defense News*, 22 May 2000.

Chapter 3

1 One particularly useful article on the history of ESDP is 'Towards a European Crisis Reaction Force', *Military Technology*, vol. 24, issue 4, 2000, pp. 44–53.

2 'EU Unveils Plans for a Rapid-Reaction Disaster Force', *Defence News*, 1 May 2000, p. 24.

3 *The Military Balance 2000–2001*, p. 35.

4 Gilles Andréani, 'Why Institutions Matter', *Survival*, vol. 42, Summer 2000, p. 81.

5 Annex 1 to Annex IV, 'Presidency Progress Report to

the Helsinki European Council on Strengthening the Common European Policy on Security and Defence', Presidency Conclusions, Helsinki European Council, 10 and 11 December 1999, pp. 17–19.

[6] *Strategic Survey 2000–2001*, p. 103.

[7] Gilles Andréani, Christoph Bertram and Charles Grant, *Europe's Military Revolution* (London: Centre for European Reform, and Paris: Institute for Security Studies, Western European Union, February 2001).

[8] 'Martti Ahtisaari Holds News Conference with Other EU Leaders Following US–EU Summit', 17 December 1999, FDCH Political Transcripts.

[9] Alain Richard press conference remarks, available on EU website (ue.eu.int), under title 'Réunion informelle des ministres de la Défense UE/ Etats tiers (15 + 15 et 15 + 6)' – Conférence de presse de MM. Richard et Solana (Bruxelles, le 21 Novembre 2000).

[10] David S. Yost, 'The NATO Capabilities Gap and the European Union', *Survival*, vol. 42, Winter 2000–01, p. 98.

[11] *Strategic Survey 2000–2001*, p. 104.

[12] Available at ue.eu.int/pesc/ military/en/CCC.htm

[13] *Ibid.*

[14] 'Meet your new European army', *The Economist*, 25 November 2000, pp. 57–63.

[15] See the Adelphi Paper by Dr Hans-Christian Hagman on this issue (in press).

[16] *Strategic Survey 2000–2001*, p. 104.

[17] Interview with the author, IISS, London, 23 March 2000.

[18] Peter Schmidt, 'ESDI: "Separable but not Separate" ', *NATO Review*, vol. 48, Spring/ Summer 2000, p. 12.

[19] 'Rapport de la présidence sur la politique européenne de sécurité et de défense', available on the website of the French EU presidency (www.presidence-eu). Page one refers to autonomous capacities and Annexe VII refers to access guarantees. On Turkey, see Ian Black, 'Turkey Resists Demand for EU Deal with NATO', *The Guardian*, 16 December 2000.

[20] Rudolf Scharping, 'Fähig zum Handeln', *Die Zeit*, 20 March 2000.

[21] 'Germany Commits to Join EU Crisis Force', *Defence News*, 3 July 2000, p. 24.

[22] 'Defence Force for Europe "Could Take 10 Years" ', *Daily Telegraph*, 30 March 2000.

[23] Interview with the author, Ministry of Defence, London, 14 June 2000.

[24] Interview with the author, Czech Foreign Ministry, Prague, 14 February 2000.

[25] Interview with the author, Polish Embassy, London, 10 December 1999.

[26] Strategic Concept, NATO Washington Summit, April 1999.

[27] 'NATO Military Doctrine Sets Goals for Force Structure', *Defence News*, 12 June 2000, p. 8.

[28] Interview with the author, Auswärtiges Amt, 23 May 2000.

[29] Strategic Concept, NATO Washington Summit, April 1999, p. 15.

[30] Interview with the author, Bundestag, Berlin, 3 December 1999.

[31] Interview with the author, Ministry of Defence, London, 14 June 2000.

9 May 2000.

[34] Interview with the author,
French Embassy, London,
24 March 2000.

[1] Presidency Report to the
Göteborg European Council on
ESDP, Brussels, 11 June 2001,
online pdf version, p. 4, available
at http://eu2001.se/static/eng/
pdf/rapport_0612.pdf.

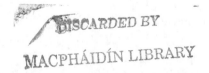